Understanding Art

To Dr. Susan Carter, great professor.

Understanding Art

Hendrik Willem Van Loon's *How to Look at Pictures*

Edited and Introduced by
Daniel Gutierrez-Sandoval

Understanding Art:
Hendrick Willem Van Loon's *How to Look at Pictures*

All Rights Reserved © 2013 by Policy Studies Organization

Westphalia Press
An imprint of Policy Studies Organization
dgutierrezs@ipsonet.org

All rights reserved. No part of this book may be reproduced or transmitted in any form or by any means graphic, electronic, or mechanical, including photocopying, recording, taping, or by any information storage or retrieval system, without the permission in writing from the publisher.

For information:
Westphalia Press
1527 New Hampshire Ave., N.W.
Washington, D.C. 20036

ISBN-13: 978-0944285749
ISBN-10: 0944285740

Updated material and comments on this edition can be found at the Policy Studies Organization website:
http://www.ipsonet.org

INTRODUCTION TO THE NEW EDITION

HENDRIK Willem van Loon was born in the Netherlands and came to America to earn his B.A. at Cornell in 1905. He later taught at Cornell and became an American citizen in 1919. He was a voluminous writer, as only a partial list of his titles illustrates:

- *The Fall of the Dutch Republic*, 1913, Houghton Mifflin
- *The Rise of the Dutch Kingdom*, 1915, Doubleday Page
- *The Golden Book of the Dutch Navigators*, 1916, Century
- *A Short History of Discovery: From the Earliest Times to the Founding of Colonies in the American Continent*, 1917, David McKay
- *Ancient Man: the Beginning of Civilizations*, 1920, Boni and Liveright
- *The Story of Mankind*, 1921, Boni and Liveright
- *The Story of the Bible*, 1923, Boni and Liveright
- *The Story of Wilbur the Hat*, 1925, Boni and Liveright
- *Tolerance*, 1925, Boni and Liveright
- *The Liberation of Mankind: the story of man's struggle for the right to think*, 1926, Boni and Liveright
- *America: The Story of America from the very beginning up to the present*, 1927, Boni and Liveright
- *Adriaen Block*, 1928, Block Hall
- *Multiplex man, or the Story of Survival through Invention*, 1928, Jonathan Cape
- *Life and Times of Peter Stuyvesant*, 1928, Henry Holt
- *Man the Miracle Maker*, 1928, Horace Liveright

- *R. v. R.: the Life and Times of Rembrandt van Rijn*, 1930, Horace Liveright
- *If the Dutch Had Kept Nieuw Amsterdam,* in *If, Or History Rewritten*, edited by J. C. Squire, 1931, Simon and Schuster
- *Van Loon's Geography: The Story of the World We Live In*, 1932, Simon and Schuster
- *An Elephant Up a Tree*, 1933, Simon and Schuster
- *An Indiscreet Itinerary or How the Unconventional Traveler Should See*, 1933, Harcourt, Brace
- *The Home of Mankind: the story of the world we live in*, 1933, George G. Harrap
- *The story of inventions: Man, the Miracle Maker*, 1934, Horace Liveright
- *Ships: and How They Sailed the Seven Seas (5000 B.C.-A.D.1935),* 1935, Simon and Schuster
- *Around the World With the Alphabet*, 1935, Simon and Schuster
- *Air-Storming: A Collection of 40 Radio Talks*, 1935, Harcourt, Brace
- *A World Divided is a World Lost*, 1935, Cosmos
- *The Songs We Sing* (with Grace Castagnetta), 1936, Simon and Schuster
- *The Arts* (illustrations by Grace Castagnetta), 1937, Simon and Schuster
- *Christmas Carols* (with Grace Castagnetta), 1937, Simon and Schuster
- *Observations on the mystery of print and the work of Johann Gutenberg*, 1937, Book Manufacturer's Institute/New York Times
- *Our Battle: Being One Man's Answer to "My Battle" by Adolf Hitler*, 1938, Simon and Schuster
- *How to Look at Pictures: a Short History of Painting*, 1938, National Committee for Art Appreciation
- *Folk Songs of Many Lands* (with Grace Castagnetta), 1938, Simon and Schuster
- *The Last of the Troubadours: The Life and Music of Carl Michael Bellman 1740-1795* (with Grace Castagnetta), 1939, Simon and Schuster

- *The Songs America Sings* (with Grace Castagnetta), 1939, Simon and Schuster
- *My School Books*,[1] 1939, E. I. du Pont de Nemours
- *Invasion*, 1940, Harcourt, Brace
- *The Story of the Pacific*, 1940, George G. Harrap
- *The Life and Times of Johann Sebastian Bach*, 1940, Simon and Schuster
- *Good Tidings* (with Grace Castegnetta), 1941, American Artists Group
- *Van Loon's Lives*, 1942, Simon and Schuster
- *The Message of the Bells* (with Grace Castagnetta), 1942, New York Garden City
- *Fighters for Freedom: the Life and Times of Thomas Jefferson and Simon Bolivar*, 1943, Dodd, Mead & Co.
- *The Life and Times of Scipio Fulhaber*, Chef de Cuisine, 1943
- *Report to Saint Peter, upon the kind of world in which Hendrik Willem van Loon spent the first years of his life* - an unfinished, posthumously published autobiography, 1947, Simon and Schuster

The scope of his titles is daunting, but perhaps this book is a fair representation of his work, because it so clearly relies on his strong opinions. A critic in the New York Times remarked, "When Hendrik Willem van Loon writes history, you can be certain of getting both plenty of history and plenty of van Loon." The book was published at the urging of Eleanor Roosevelt and a short-lived voluntary national committee for art appreciation she encouraged. Their intention was to reproduce paintings of Matisse, Van Gogh, Gainsborough, Picasso, Gauguin, Titian, and other greats and make them widely available at a small cost to the general public. While the committee vanished, one benefit of its work is this highly readable if controversial view of art.

Daniel Gutierrez-Sandoval

HOW TO LOOK AT PICTURES

How to Look at Pictures

A SHORT HISTORY OF PAINTING

BY HENDRIK WILLEM VAN LOON

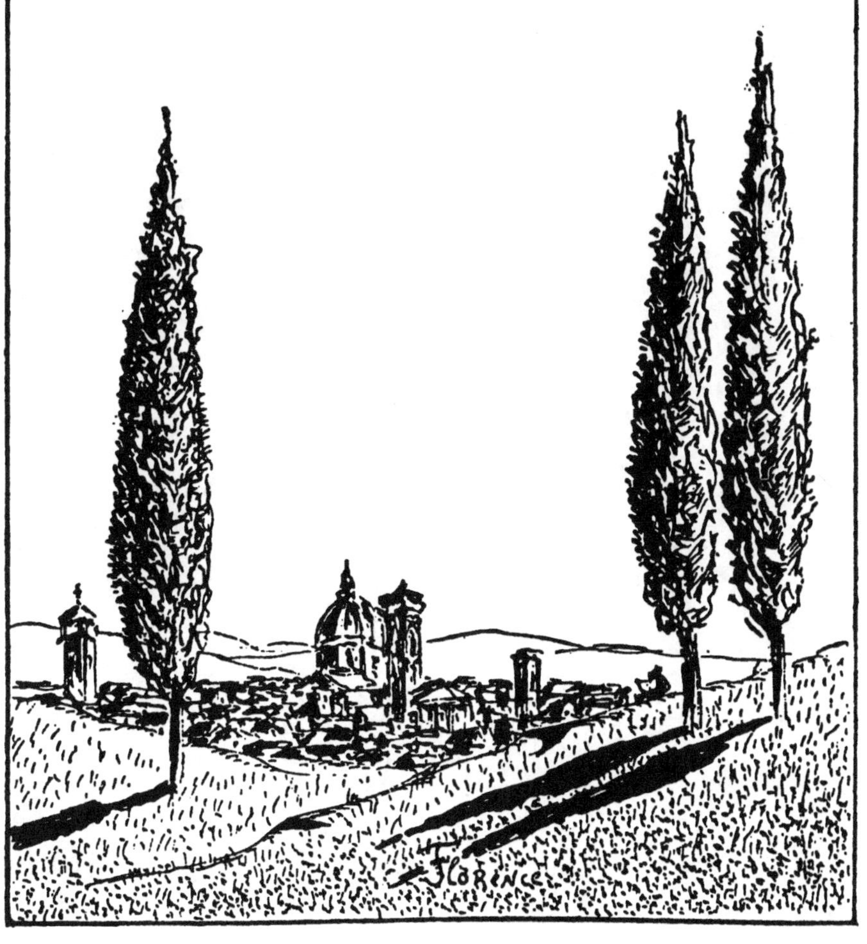

FOREWORD

To the Reader:

No, this is not (if I may use a rather vulgar expression) a rehash of what I wrote in that much longer book which I published only a short time ago and in which I made an attempt to gather all the arts together into one single volume. I would not blame you, however, if you thought so, for that sort of thing has been done before and sometimes quite successfully.

But in this instance it is rather the other way around and it may well be that the tail will prove to wag the dog. For when I had at last written finis *to the endless labor connected with that ponderous tome, I found that while engaged upon this endless task I had learned so many new things that my entire outlook upon the different arts had gradually been changed. I could, of course, have thrown everything I had written into Long Island Sound (it is conveniently near, right outside my window), but there were my publishers who eagerly wanted to know when they could begin to print. And there was I, so hopelessly tired after four years of the hardest work I had ever done, that I just lacked the courage to do it all over again.*

What you will therefore find in this little book is my outlook upon the world of the painter's art as it was developed during the years I was engaged upon the task of preparing the much longer volume which preceded this opusculum *by about half a year. I think I owe you these few words of explanation. The rest of what I have to say you will find in the following pages.*

Hendrik Willem van Loon

Old Greenwich, Conn.
January 8, 1938

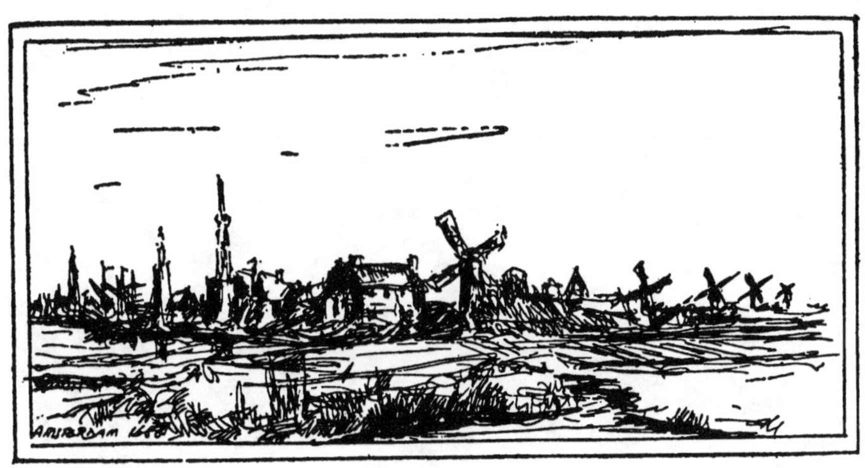

CONTENTS

ILLUSTRATIONS

I

WHAT DOES THE PAINTER REALLY TRY TO DO?

I SUPPOSE that now it can be told. But when I began work upon my big volume on the arts, I experienced the greatest difficulty when I finally had to give a concrete definition of the art of the painter and what the painter really is and what he tries to do.

My first impulse was to say that a painter was a creature who tried to communicate his ideas to others by means of his pictures and that it may be said of him—and often is—that he "told you a story in a visible form." But such a statement might very easily have led to all sorts of misunderstandings. For right away it would have been interpreted as an encouragement of just the sort of painting of which all true artists most heartily disapprove—the magazine-cover sort of picture that tells a sweet and futile story—the pretty and sentimental Christmas supplement hanging on the wall of Aunt Amy's guest-room, showing a little girl saying her prayers in company with her pet kitten, or a faithful old Saint Bernard digging a lovely maiden out of the snow.

And so I avoided that expression, for it was bound to have been misinterpreted. Yet that is exactly what the painter does and what the sculptor does and what the composer does and what the novelist does. Each one in his own way tries to convey unto others an impression of something he himself has seen or experienced. The painter looks at a landscape which strikes him by its harmonious simplicity or by its rugged disorganization. It does not matter what it is, for beauty and ugliness are very relative terms in the artist's studio. It is enough that it has a certain quality which appeals to the painter's emotions and makes him reach out for his pencil or his brush. The rest is no concern of his. He can leave that to the critics and the public, for his job is done the moment his picture is finished.

Had he been a composer, he would have tried to tell us about his experience by means of sound.

Had he been a poet, he would have endeavored to do so by means of words.

Being a painter, he was obliged to use the medium most familiar to his own particular sort of talent—the medium of color and line. And that is really all there is to the problem of "Why do people paint pictures?" They do so because they must. And all art that is not the result of such a divine *must* is bad art.

If you can grasp this simple fact and never lose sight of it, you will find that it is an unfailing key to practically every mystery connected with the pictorial arts. Just ask yourself, "What did this man want to tell me?" Then try to see that man as he must have been in the age in which he lived, or, in other words, try to see him completely detached from any modern considerations, for you can't mix 1938 and 1438 or 638 B.C. without getting everything completely out of focus. Then ask yourself whether he seems to have been honest with himself and with his subject in the light of his own times. If he has been, you may not always like him but you will at least respect him and in a world so full of a number of people and therefore so full of a number of tastes, respect is about as much as any of us can hope for. And respect—in art as well as in life—will often lead to a lasting affection. So that you can never really tell what will happen and since a little bit of understanding is the true spice of life, even the dullest of our museums may prove to be an unexpected treasure-chest of glorious adventure.

Let me go briefly back to the beginning of things. It will help you to understand what I am driving at.

Look at the oldest pictures that have survived. During the last few years they have so often been reproduced that you can easily find them somewhere. The exact date at which they were made is not known, but they must have been painted during the end of the last of the great glacial periods when the snow fields of Europe were slowly retreating toward the north and when the southern part of Europe was once more becoming inhabitable.

The "human race" that followed in the wake of the ice fields was still in a very primitive state of development and the architect (the oldest of all artists next to the manufacturer of personal adornments) had not yet made his appearance to show his customers how to build themselves a house. The few wanderers in this wilderness camped out as best they could in those caves which the ice had dug into the soft stone of the mountains of southern France and northern Spain. And behold! as soon as they had put their rather uncomfortable houses in order, there seem to have been a few members of the clan who had to give concrete expression to some of their ideas by means of pictures.

To us, who can go through life without ever seeing a wild animal, these are very curious pictures. We don't quite see as these artists did, but that only means that we ourselves may be wrong. For wild animals were by far the most important factor in the life of prehistoric man. They were at once his most dangerous enemies and the source of most of his supplies, from mammoth steaks to the needles which he made himself out of the reindeer's antlers, and therefore he knew them infinitely better than we can ever hope to do.

A great many of these early pictures representing the wild animals of ten thousand years ago have survived, and they show us that the men of the Stone Age, whom we had always imagined as complete savages, were much better observers and therefore much better draughtsmen than many of the generations that lived in a much more recent age. What became of them we do not know, but their work deserves our very close attention, for these poor, shivering savages had somehow got hold of the one true principle that underlies all good art: Have something to say; say it with as little waste motion as possible; and then stop talking.

At some date completely unknown to us the curtain descends upon the art of the cavemen. When it rises again, behold! we see a landscape very different from that of the bleak northern wilderness. For now we find ourselves in the peaceful and fertile valley of the Nile. Prehistoric man had been a hunter, leading an active life and

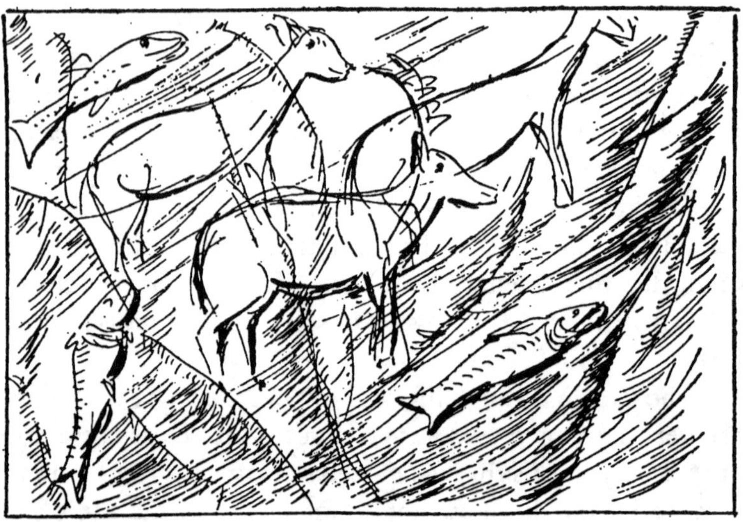

The observation of the prehistoric painter was better than that of many modern artists.

depending for his safety and success upon the quickness of his eye and the sharpness of his powers of observation. The Egyptian, on the other hand, like his contemporaries in the valley of the Euphrates and the Tigris, was a patient tiller of the soil, a placid creature who was born, who raised his crops of grain and his crops of children and who lived and died—generation after generation, century after century—on the very same spot, until he seemed almost as imperishable (and about as much alive) as those mummies which he hid in the sands of the deserts.

Being the subject of what today we would call a totalitarian state (Russia, Germany, Italy), he had very little life of his own. His architecture (except for his own mud hut) was a wholesale architecture. His temples were wholesale affairs. The tombs of his kings and queens were wholesale monuments to the glory of some particularly successful dictator. And so was his art. It was a wholesale art and an official art. But like the art of the early caveman, it showed a tremendous power of observation. Whether the Egyptian sculptor or painter tried to show us man or beast, he gave evidence of being thoroughly familiar with his subject. He was as yet completely ignorant of the rules of perspective, but when you study his art you will soon notice that this so-called absence of perspective does not in the least interfere with your enjoyment of the subject. No more than it does with the delight you will derive from Chinese and Japanese paintings which are also completely lacking in that particular sort of perspective of which the western artist has almost made a fetish.

Of course there are other details in this art of the Egyptians which will make you feel that you are dealing with something that is quite foreign to our modern way of looking at things. For the Egyptian masters (as well as their colleagues of Babylonia and every other part of western Asia) had not yet learned to give expression to the human face. They undoubtedly tried as hard as they could to depict the emotions and often they succeeded in conveying certain attitudes of fear or joy or apprehension by the actions of the body, by the gestures of the hands or the position of the legs, but they almost invariably failed when it came to facial expression.

It was much easier to achieve satisfactory results with animals than with human beings, for animals, who live much more with their bodies than we do, can express themselves much more clearly by means of their bodies than we do.

I cannot go into too much detail about the pictorial art of the people of the Nile. It will probably always remain a special delicacy for a very small number of true connoisseurs. But unless you have at least paid some attention to the art of the valley of the Nile, you will never understand that which came after. For the Egyptians were the teachers of the Greeks and the Greeks in turn taught us most of what we know. Even in the days of our grandfathers the notion existed that the Greeks had been men of such singular genius that, like their own Goddess Athena, they had sprung fully armed and equipped from the head of the great god Zeus.

Unfortunately in art as well as in nature (and in our own lives) nothing ever came forth from nothing and there can be no pupil without a teacher. Now and then some strange creature arises who seems to have been born to confound this rule. But invariably, when we go far enough back, we discover that he too got his original inspiration from some other source. It was not until some fifty years ago, when we became aware of the lost civilizations of Crete and those other islands which form a connecting link between Asia and Africa and Europe, that we began to realize how the artistic principles of the Egyptians had found their way from the valley of the Nile to that small peninsula (then called Hellas) inhabited for a thousand years by immigrants from northern Europe. And today we know definitely that the Greeks only continued what the Egyptians had begun, thirty centuries before.

Painting is essentially an indoor art, used to embellish the rooms of our homes and public buildings. I therefore have always doubted whether the Greeks themselves thought very much about it or held it in high esteem. Both the Greeks and the Romans were essentially an out-of-door sort of people. The climate (then apparently a great deal milder than now) allowed them to spend most of their waking hours out in the streets and market-places. Their houses (very simple affairs) were merely what the home of the average modern Italian is to him today—a place where he sleeps and eats and raises his family and keeps his wife out of harm's way, but where for the rest he wastes just as little time as possible.

As the free citizens of both Athens and Rome lived on the labor of their slaves (these slaves were their invested capital and their machines), they had a lot of spare time which they could devote to politics and festive religious processions and dramatic performances, to sports and to warfare (then also a kind of sport and much less dangerous than modern automobiling). But all of these were again out-of-door affairs and when the board of aldermen met, it convened on the grassy slope of a hill and not in a solemn chamber decorated with WPA murals and the pictures of defunct mayors and aldermen. The painter, therefore, although he existed, did not enjoy a great demand upon his services and remained an obscure figure in comparison with the architects and the sculptors, who, working out in the open, fulfilled a very essential need. From this however we should not draw the conclusion that the Greeks were indifferent to color. On the contrary. The Greeks from the days of Homer and Pericles were as crazy about color as are their modern descendants when they go in for patriotic pictures about their king or whoever happens to be their ruler at the moment. All those noble marble statues that now appeal to us by their very austerity were originally covered with a heavy layer of brilliant reds and blues and yellows and greens.

It follows that the Greek painter must have known how to handle color, but in a way that would have been far from pleasing to our modern taste. He was familiar also with the principles of drawing, for Greek civilization was essentially a civilization of pottery, just as ours is a civilization of glass and tin. Without a profound knowledge of drawing, it would have been impossible to cover all this pottery with the intricate scenes and designs that give it such a fascinating quality and that accounted for its popularity all over the ancient world. But the slaves who were responsible for these designs and these pictures of Gods and Goddesses engaged in mortal combat, were taken entirely for granted, as we usually take for granted those artists who devise the labels for the tin cans containing our tomatoes, our pea soup or our baked beans and who work in a haze of complete anonymity.

This general feeling of indifference toward the men who devised those marvelous pictures on that old Greek earthenware seems to have extended also to those masters who specialized in murals. Murals were to be found in the courtyards of all the better-class houses of both the Greeks and the Romans. However they were placed there more to amuse and interest the wives and the children than the master of the house, and as a result most of these paintings have a sort of "nursery quality" which may amuse us but which rarely interests us

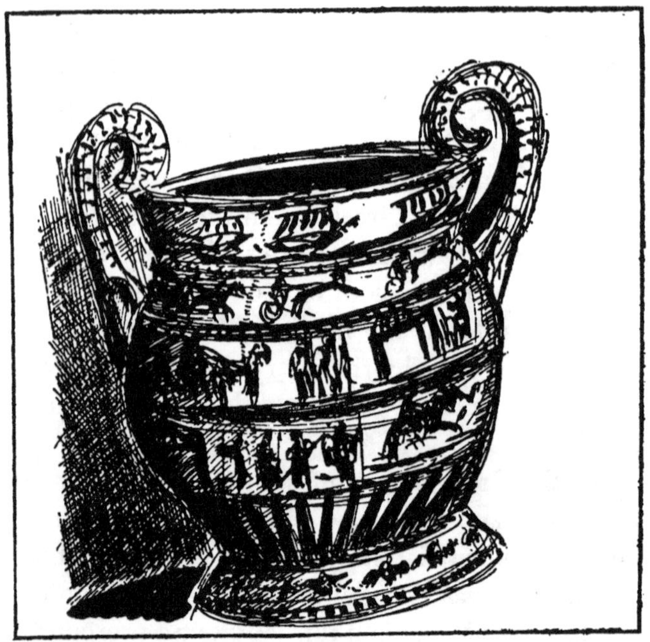

Designs on their pottery show us that the Greek painters were excellent draughtsmen.

except as a direct historical curiosity. All this you will observe for yourself when you go to the buried cities of Pompeii and Herculaneum. The Muses had been very generous to the ancient Helenes but painting, alas, was their step-child. They treated it kindly and occasionally gave it a pat on the back. But they never regarded it as one of their own.

In most histories of art there is a special chapter devoted to the paintings of the early Christian era. I therefore should mention the subject, but properly speaking there never was such a thing as "early Christian painting." What we call by that name was in reality "late pagan painting." For the early Christians, almost without exception, belonged to the class of the slaves and of the very humble, who had never developed any art of their own. Therefore when at last they began to organize into definite communities and for safety's sake began to hold meetings in the deserted stone quarries around Rome, they had to hire either the regular old pagan painters to ornament these subterranean passages for them or none at all. And it was quite natural that these craftsmen, having been trained in the traditions of the older Roman civilization, should have continued to paint the same heroes they had always painted, except that now the heroes got new names.

This led to curious results. Until the fifth century of our era, the Christ remains a beardless young man, sometimes appearing in the guise of Hermes or Orpheus and at other times playing the role of Apollo, the sun-god, whose head since time immemorial had been surrounded by the disc that represented the shining sun, for the word *halo* is really Greek for "disc."

But after the middle of the fifth century, when Rome ceased to be the capital of the world and Constantinople (Byzantium) took its place and when emperors and officials with long ornamental beards succeeded their clean-shaven Roman predecessors, the Christ figure, too, was given that beard without which today we would hardly recognize it. To have represented him smooth-shaven would have been a terrible heresy in the eyes of these Eastern potentates. It would have made him look like a slave or, worse still, like an actor.

By the same token, these early Christians would not imagine Mary the Queen of Heaven unless they associated her with the wife of their worldly emperor; wherefore in the pictures of the early Middle Ages she always appears as a very great lady, surrounded by a host of servants, dressed in all the splendor of the imperial court.

This is a good occasion to show you how, in all the arts, traditions will survive long after they have lost their meaning. For thousands of years the Greeks and Romans had believed that the road to the

Hereafter was a dark and dismal river called the Styx. And behold! in the Catacombs the souls of the blessed are shown us proceeding to their eternal reward across a dark and dismal sea, filled with all the monsters of the older pagan mythology.

I could give you many other examples to show the almost incredible power-to-survive of old traditions. During these first five centuries (and even after) you will never come across a representation of the crucifixion, the one subject which during the Middle Ages was to play such a very important part in Christian art. Even after they had been converted for almost half a dozen generations, these early Christians still associated their Saviour with the idea of Hermes, the good shepherd of their heathenish days, on whose Festive Day the handsomest young man of the town used to carry a young lamb on his shoulders around the walls of his city, that the next year might be a fortunate one. The idea that this noble looking youth should have died on the cross like any common slave was unbearable to them, and the Christ, in their eyes, remained the Good Shepherd.

By the same token, the unfortunate Phaeton of mythological days, whose clumsy handling of the sun-chariot had almost caused our earth to go up in smoke and ashes, survived as the prophet Elijah mounting toward Heaven. And so in every possible way the old pagan form of painting survived until the last of the unreconstructed pagans had long since withdrawn from a world which seemed to have lost all its former charm and joy, and then the time had at last come for a purely Christian form of art to find expression in terms that were also essentially Christian.

But when this happened, it found its expression in a new medium, the medium we know as mosaics. Mosaics (so-called after the Muses) are a sort of painting done with beads of marble or glass, usually colored in white, gold, blue, and green. You rarely see good mosaics nowadays. The few remaining families who can do that sort of work (most of them Italians) find but little demand for their labors. Mosaics are not like pictures. You can't transport them. They have to be built right into the walls of your building and they are as much a part of the general architectural scheme as the statues on the façade. It is of course possible to transport the whole of such walls, just as it has proved possible to remove entire temples from Asia Minor and Greece to Europe and America. But nowadays there are few nations that still allow themselves to be plundered that way and therefore, if you want to see really good mosaics, you must travel to such out-of-the-way places as the town of Ravenna (that dreadful village on the Adriatic that was the New York of the fifth century) or to Venice. You will also find them in a few of the earlier churches of Rome and other Italian cities, and today (since they have been purged of their heavy layers of whitewash by the new Turkish rulers) you can also study them in Saint Sophia in Constantinople.

Mosaics are not a form of art which is apt to play much of a role in our own American civilization. Yet one should know something about them for they are part of the bridge that connects the craft of the painter, as practiced by the ancients, with that of their medieval successors. And since now at last we reach a more familiar period of history and begin to catch an occasional glimpse of a sort of art that speaks our own language (just as Chaucer spoke our own language, even though it is not always entirely clear to us), we had better bid farewell to the preliminary studies and come down to the matter we really want to discuss.

2

THE ROMANESQUE PERIOD

A new and vigorous civilization begins slowly to emerge from the ruins of the classical world and the architect reappears upon the scene, but the painter lags behind, as there is really very little practical demand for his services.

WITH our modern eyes we see the artist as a lusty fellow who paints what he sees or pretends to see—how and when and where he happens to see it. Thereupon we can like what he has done or not, as we ourselves feel inclined. That is really no concern of his, for he is free to paint as he likes and if we don't happen to like it, well, that is just too bad for us. It won't make him lose any sleep or cause him to skip a few of his scanty meals. He is a free agent. He recognizes no other master but his own artistic conscience and that is that!

Alas! those few painters who had survived the downfall of the old Roman and Greek civilizations were not as fortunate as their brethren of today. In the first place, they had absolutely no liberty of action. The Council of Nicaea in the year 325 (the first general council of the Christian Church ever to be held) had laid down the rule that "the subject of a picture was not a matter to be left to the imagination of the painter, but that it must be subject to the traditions and the legislation of the Church."

But even if the painter had been free in the choice of his subjects, what could he have done with his pictures once they were finished? Who would have bought them? Who would even have accepted them as a gift? To understand how completely the painter was "out of the picture" during the early part of the Middle Ages, try to imagine the world in which he lived.

The old order of things was gone as completely as it is gone today in Russia and in Spain. The cities had been destroyed by the endless invasions of those eastern barbarians who, being nomads and accustomed to the wide open spaces, had hated cities as cordially as our own Indians of three hundred years ago used to hate the enclosures which the white man had built in the Canadian and New England wilderness. The roads had fallen into neglect. The bridges were gone beyond any hope of repair. The sea was no longer safe, after the international policeman (the Roman legionary) had disappeared from the scene. Hunger and illness and despair had decimated the population of southern Europe. Here and there, a mere handful of people eked out a miserable existence among the ruins of those cities which only a few centuries before had been as important as London or Paris is today. In Rome the population had dwindled from more than a million people to less than twenty thousand. In certain Roman cities of southern France, the entire populace now lived huddled together in the old circus. Imagine the people of Cambridge, Massachusetts, having to find a refuge in the Harvard Stadium or the inhabitants of New Haven being obliged to take shelter in the Yale Bowl, and you will understand how thoroughly the work of demolition had been done. A sensitive person (and the artist is apt to be at least "artistically sensitive") had literally no place to go. The new masters of Europe (as tough a set of gangsters as ever played a role in history) were much too busy fighting each other for the spoils of the old Empire to care about any forms of art. And so the artists (all of them—not merely the painters) had to wait until some new form of civilization should arise out of the ruins of the old one before they could once more hope to ply their ancient trade.

When during the fifth and sixth centuries monastic orders began to make their appearance, the artists could occasionally hide themselves and their dreams behind the sheltering walls of those religious establishments. But most of the monks were the product of their own time and their taste, as a rule, was that of the barbarian chieftains whose protection and favor they needed in order to conquer Europe for the Christian faith.

This era is usually known as the Romanesque period. Such historical divisions are of course entirely artificial. The Romanesque period did not suddenly begin in the ninth century nor did it abruptly come to an end in the thirteenth century, when it was replaced by Gothic, which thereupon endured until it was pushed off the stage by the Renaissance which succeeded it during the first half of the fifteenth century. All these periods overlap. They last much longer in one country than in another. They begin much earlier in one part of the world than in another. And ofttimes they survive for centuries after they are supposed to have come to an end. Today we are building Romanesque churches in Chicago and we are mixing Gothic with our skyscrapers in New York. The best known church in Boston is pure Romanesque and all our American towns are as full of Renaissance buildings as they are full of Greek temples, the latter a very favorite style with the directors of our banks because, I suppose, the Greek style is somehow supposed to suggest an element of purity and integrity. As for Washington, to give you a concrete example which you can study with your own eyes, the city is such a hopeless mixture of practically every style, from early Egyptian to late Baroque, that there is no room left for anything that might reflect the architectural genius of our own day—the more is the pity!

However, we badly need a few definite dates for the sake of our faulty memories and therefore we use the expression Romanesque to describe the architecture (or rather, the spirit which inspired that particular form of architecture) which followed upon the disappearance of the old Roman and early Byzantine styles and which preceded the introduction of Gothic during the middle of the thirteenth century.

As most people are almost completely unaware of the existence of that eastern half of the ancient Roman Empire, which survived the downfall of Rome by almost a thousand years (Columbus was seven years old when Constantinople was taken by the Turks), I shall mention it only briefly. To us, the Byzantines are chiefly important as the people who gave their Russian neighbors their first notions about civilization, about religion and about art. After the downfall of the last of the Russian Caesars (remember that "Czar" is the same word as

"Caesar," if you want another example of the tenacity of ancient traditions) some twenty years ago, a great deal of Russian art was lost or stolen and found its way to Europe and to America. Many people therefore caught their first glimpse of Byzantine art when they were

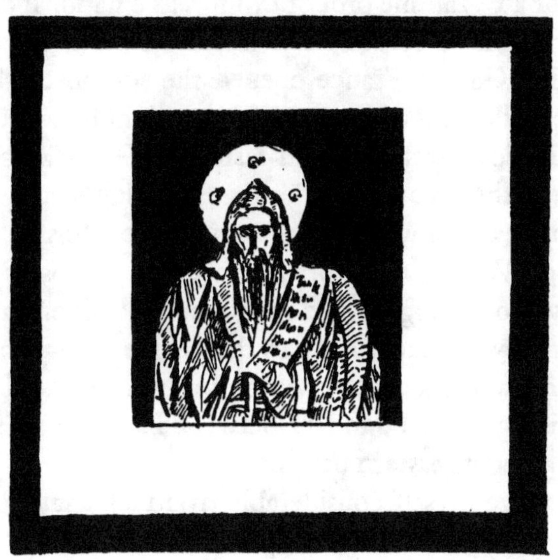

The art of Byzantium and Russia, being a "prescribed" form of art, went into a dead-alley and became fossilized.

offered some fine Russian ikons for sale—"guaranteed genuine and formerly owned by one of the grand-dukes." As a rule they failed to interest the prospective buyer, and small wonder. For the ikons were visible reminders of that curious rule for the graphic arts as laid down by the Council of Nicaea, some sixteen hundred years ago. It required, you recall, that the painter in the choice of his subjects let himself be guided not by his own inclinations but by the law and the tradition of the Church.

Byzantine architecture, like Byzantine painting, rarely influenced the people of western Europe. The spirit of the East was completely foreign to that of the West. In the eastern part of Europe an old and moribund civilization was slowly and painfully coming to its logical end. In the West, a dozen new nations, crude and vulgar but full of the lust of life, were beginning to feel their own strength. They had as much use for a Byzantine order of things as a national convention of either Democrats or Republicans would have for the procedure with which the King of France opened the session of the Estates General in Versailles in the year 1789. They might be willing to learn a few technical tricks from those old-fashioned Greek architects, but that was as far as they would go. For the rest, they seem to have felt that they would have to work out their own problems as best suited their own needs. We can therefore bid farewell to those Byzantines, ceremoniously proceeding toward their inevitable doom, and devote ourselves from now on exclusively to the people who inhabited that part of Europe that is situated between the Atlantic and the Vistula, the river that is really the boundary between Europe and Asia, since Russia begins along its eastern banks.

I could here save myself considerable trouble by saying that Romanesque art offered very little scope to the talents of the painter, and then proceed to the Gothic period when all the graphic arts experienced a tremendous boost. But you would quite naturally ask, "Why was that so?" and I think that it is better to answer that question before it has even been asked. Remember—even I get to be a little boresome in stressing this point—remember that art, in order to be healthy and normal, must fulfill some practical role in society. The worst part of unemployment is not merely the absence of any regular source of income for its victims, but rather that terrible sense of despair which takes hold of their minds when they are beginning to feel that they are no longer "a necessary part of the community." A painter or a sculptor or a musician who must exist on a spiritual dole and who no longer is inspired by the conviction that what he does is really of tremendous importance to at least a few of his fellowmen—such a painter or sculptor or musician had better be dead, for he has become that which no honest man wants to be, a superfluous luxury. Hence painters and architects and musicians and authors and fiddling virtuosos or swing players will appear upon the scene when they are needed and they will begin to disappear when the need has ceased to be. And the plain fact in the case is that the Romanesque period did not really need the painter. The very nature of the Romanesque style militated against the development of any of the pictorial arts. In the first place, these Romanesque churches were very small. You might compare them to the chapels built early in the eighteenth century somewhere in the province of Quebec by a few courageous French priests. Why should they have tried to erect anything larger? Their parishioners were few in number. There were no stonemasons who knew their trade. How could they, and why should they, have tried to build themselves a vast structure, able to hold a thousand worshippers, when their congregations at best counted only fifty or sixty souls and why should they have bothered to cover the walls with pictures which none of these benighted heathen could have understood?

Furthermore, during the tenth and eleventh centuries, northern Europe was only very slowly being converted to Christianity. Many of these early churches had to be fortresses as well as places of worship, for at any moment they might be attacked by pirates or be exposed to a native uprising. The walls had to be very thick, while the doors and windows had to be small. Glass was practically unknown and not even the king in his palace could always allow himself the luxury of a glass window. When it grew cold, he filled that small opening in the wall with a couple of skins while he sat and shivered in front of his open fire, for he was not spoiled by too much "comfort." As a rule he was dead anyway before he had reached the early forties.

These Romanesque churches therefore had a lot of wall-space but nobody knew what to do with it. One could break the monotony of the walls with a few statues, and statues were therefore quite common, both inside and outside of the Romanesque churches. And then came the demand for color, for no form of civilization can exist for very long without some bright spots of color. But again, color was scarce, for the art of making different pigment is a very delicate one and becomes quite easily forgotten, once the men who knew it have been killed or have starved to death.

There were of course those tapestries, which an occasional traveler had brought back all the way from Constantinople. There were a few odds and ends of silk which some pious sailor had found in the cabin of a Moslem pirate ship, and here and there in some lonely monastery there lived a few ancient craftsmen still vaguely familiar with the painter's art as practiced in the days of the Romans. But they were now devoting themselves to the less ambitious task of embellishing holy books with pictures—with miniatures—that the mighty of this earth, who could neither read nor write, should at least know something about the story of their Saviour. Whenever the occasion demanded it, these bookish fellows were provided with the necessary paints (some of these colors, especially red, were way beyond the purse of anyone but a ruling monarch) and they were then set to work on the walls of the churches, but judging by what survives of those early periods, such occasions were very rare and these men could therefore spend most of their time working away at their miniatures.

Today the name "miniature painting" is often applied to those very small portraits painted on ivory which were so highly esteemed by our grandparents and for which we seem to have lost all taste, since there are very few modern craftsmen able to make a living at that sort of thing. But the miniature paintings I have in mind are the "illuminations" found in ancient books. They may at first fail to impress you, but they are worth a little trouble on your part, for once you come to understand them you will derive as much pleasure from this diminutive world as from the works of the great Italians of the eighteenth century, covering what at first glance seems to be an entire city block. And furthermore it was out of the school of miniature painters of the early Middle Ages that we got the school of the great painters of the latter half of that period.

The best of these miniatures are being more and more reproduced, and you can buy these reproductions for very little money. Get a few if you can and hang them on your bedroom wall where you can be exposed to them while dressing or choosing a necktie. It is an excellent method of getting familiar with many delightful future friends.

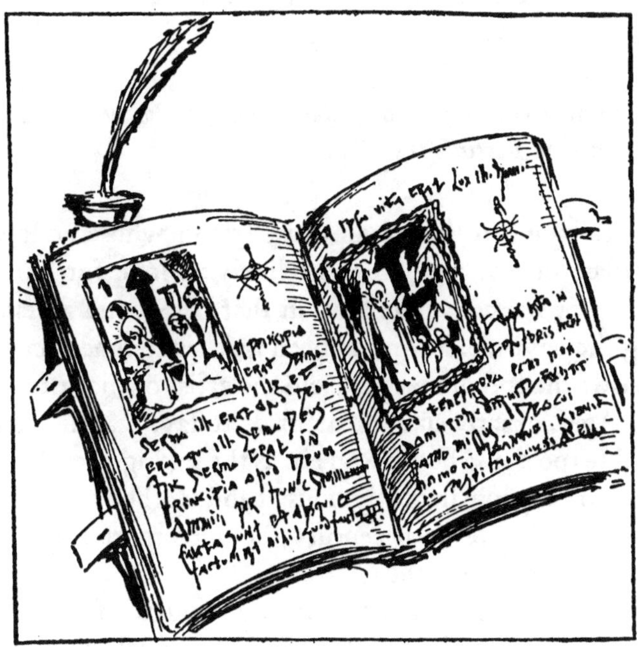

The earliest medieval painters were graduates from the older school of miniature painters.

3

THE GOTHIC ERA

1250–1450

The painter reappears upon the scene, for he has at last found a new patron—the Church.

IF YOU art trying to locate an artist friend whose address you have mislaid or lost, you are more likely to look for him in the neighborhood of Park Avenue than in that of Second Avenue—at least during the daytime. For it has been true since time immemorial that art follows the full dinner pail, and the artist of the latter half of the Middle Ages, exactly like the artist of today, was no exception to this rule. He too could not live on air, as the saying goes. He had to find a patron to keep him decently housed and clothed and fed. After the beginning of the eleventh century, he once more found such a patron and that patron was the Church.

That of course was only natural. After a struggle of a great many centuries, the Church had finally succeeded in establishing itself as the undisputed heir to the old Roman tradition of world empire. This had only been possible because the ancient ideal of some sort of super-power that could guarantee safety and peace to the whole of mankind—that ancient ideal was still so strong in most people's minds that even six centuries of complete chaos had not been able to destroy it completely. On the contrary, this long period of time had served only to make the average man all the more conscious of the absolute need for some such super-power. And therefore when a new sovereign, armed only with the sword of Faith (occasionally backed up of course by somewhat more substantial weapons) undertook to play that role of supreme judge and arbiter, it could count upon the good will and the support of a surprisingly large number of people. But in order to keep its hold upon the masses, the Church had to do two things: educate them to its own point of view and impress them with its glory and opulence.

For the Church had a very dangerous rival. In the year 800 the Pope, sorely beset by a thousand different foes, had bestowed the ancient dignity of a Roman Emperor upon that one tribal chieftain who seemed strong enough to protect the inheritance of Saint Peter against its enemies, both from the East and the West. The successors of this great monarch (whom we know as Charlemagne) had not always been as reverent in their attitude as this far-seeing and far-sighted Frankish king, and the rejuvenated Roman Empire (that Holy Roman Empire of which it was afterwards said that it had been neither holy nor Roman nor an empire) had for centuries endeavored to place itself at the head of the procession by its bold and not very well authenticated claim that it, rather than the Pope, was the true representative of the divine ideal of universal empire.

Hence the greater part of the early half of the Middle Ages (roughly speaking from the ninth until the fifteenth centuries) was filled by an unceasing struggle between these two pretenders to the role of a super-power: on the one hand the Church and on the other hand the rulers of the Holy Roman Empire. As a result, both sides looked for all the possible aid they could obtain in this endless struggle with a most dangerous rival. And the Church, being much better organized and on the whole much more intelligent in such matters than the semi-savage Franconian and Saxon and Serbian and Bohemian nobles who got themselves elected to the dignity of a Holy Roman Emperor of the German nation—the Church quite naturally availed itself of the artists as most useful allies in its endless struggle with the uncouth barbarians from across the Alps.

I am of course making all this perhaps a little too simple to be entirely within scale. The professional historian may object that the process was a little more complicated than you might conclude from this very sketchy outline. But I have only 77 pages in which to cover an awful lot of territory and in its main points this brief outline is undoubtedly true. Whether consciously or unconsciously, both sides made use of all the weapons they could lay hand on and Art, being one of the most convincing arguments in any contest (as is very well understood by our modern dictators), profited in all its forms and manifestations.

The sculptor, as we have seen, had already been able to attend to a great deal of educational work during the Romanesque period. Simple statues had been enough for the needs of a simple people. Ninety-nine percent of them were engaged in the simple pursuits of agriculture, and statuary appealed to them as it does to all primitive people. But now the world was no longer a world inhabited exclusively by farmers and country squires. The days of the great migrations belonged to an almost forgotten past. The land had been parcelled out among thousands of small but ambitious local chieftains, who as counts and dukes and barons ruled as much territory as they could safely hold against their neighbors. This so-called feudal world was no Paradise but neither was it probably quite as brutal and cruel as we have been told by the historians of the last generation. For its art tells a different tale and so does the architecture of those cities that were now once more beginning to play such a very important part in the economic and social life of a community which until then had regarded a village of two thousand people as quite a large town.

This new rise of a civic population was one of the most interesting developments of the thirteenth and fourteenth centuries and it was the immediate result of a change in the habits of the people of southern and western Europe. For almost seven centuries they had lived poverty-stricken lives. The Crusades had brought them in close contact with a civilization highly superior to their own. A little taste of luxury is apt to develop quite an appetite for the good things of this world. The rise of Venice, Genoa, Florence, Pisa, and a score of other commercial centers in Italy, followed by the equally astonishing growth of such manufacturing centers as Bruges and Ghent and the cities of the North Sea and the Baltic and the towns along the river Rhone in France—all this was evidence of that new prosperity that was once more beginning to make itself felt in every part of the old continent. As a result of all this, Europe too was no longer obliged to vegetate in a sort of economic void. Once more a steady stream of gold was beginning to trickle across a land in which for almost seven hundred years all trade had been based upon the principles of barter. And the result was a large amount of spare cash that could now be used for such non-productive purposes as painting and music.

Painting was the first of the arts to profit from the new worldly economy. Music was a close second, as I hope to tell you some time in another little book.

This particular era in our history is usually known as the age of the Gothic. The word itself is highly significant, for it was by no means meant as a compliment by the Italians who first used it. On the contrary! To the Italians of the twelfth century, the name Gothic meant something done in the style of the Goths, in the manner of those barbarians who during the third and fourth centuries had destroyed their old and cherished civilization. When these Goths (we used to say "Huns" during the World War and some of us are saying it again today)—these up and coming savages began to build a new sort of church which looked like a stone skyscraper and which followed perpendicular lines rather than the low horizontal lines of the old Romanesque churches, the Italians, considering this innovation a direct blow at their own method of building, contemptuously called it the Gothic or barbaric style. Somehow or other the term stuck and today that entire era between the thirteenth and fifteenth centuries is generally referred to as the age of the Gothic.

However, as I have already warned you, the introduction of a new style did not mean that after the year 1250 every new church became a streamline affair, with a pointed roof and arched doors and windows that took up most of the wall space. It was a question of very slow growth and development and in Italy the Gothic style never really caught a solid foothold. The Romanesque style maintained itself until it was at last replaced by the style of the Renaissance, late during the fifteenth century. But the painters could not quite escape the trend of the times, and as a result we often find them painting typically Gothic scenes on the walls of churches that were still completely Romanesque in all their structural details.

Now as you may remember, all Romanesque buildings had had heavy walls with comparatively small windows, and the interiors therefore had offered a lot of vacant space on which the painters could tell their stories. All they had to do was to cover the walls with a layer of fresh damp plaster and set to work. When the plaster and the paint dried, the job was done for all time. This fresh plaster, by the way, gave us our expression of *al fresco* painting—"painting on the fresh or *fresco* plaster."

Again I am obliged to be very brief. *Al fresco* painting was quite simple, but it took a lot of practice and routine and skill to do this sort of work well. And the preparations had to be most carefully made, for *fresco* painting was not like oil painting. Once the plaster had started to dry, you could not possibly correct your mistakes. When you use oil you can work at the same canvas for twenty years if you feel so inclined. But fresco painting either "sits," as the Dutch painters expressed it so aptly, or it does not. In the latter case you are out of luck. You have to chisel the plaster off the wall and begin all over again.

However, as there was very little money during the Middle Ages, nobody had as yet hit upon the unfortunate phrase that "time is money." And as there were always plenty of pupils (for the guilds, whatever their shortcomings, insisted upon a protracted period of apprenticeship), the master could leave the preliminary work to the little boys who worked for him and could devote all his time to his sketches, and then when everything was ready, he would roll up his sleeves, pitch in and finish his problem in record time.

In case there were no walls for him on which to work, he would have a flat wooden board covered with a thin layer of plaster. But this too was a somewhat complicated process and it remained so until the discovery of oil painting by a couple of Flemings during the first half of the fifteenth century practically did away with the unsatisfactory *al fresco* method.

There you have the general background of the painter when during the latter half of the twelfth century he emerged from the workshop of the mosaic maker and from the quiet cell of the monastery in which he had been "illuminating" his holy books. Once more he felt that there was a real demand for his labors—that he had ceased to be an entirely superfluous luxury and had got both feet back on the common ground of everyday life.

During the previous seven centuries he had lost all touch with the pagan world which had still so completely dominated the art of the early Christian Church. He had developed new types of saints. His Saviour, as I have already told you, no longer resembled a handsome Greek god. He knew the stories of the sacred Scriptures much better than the men of an earlier age. And he was now asked to tell those stories in his own terms. For that is the point of view from which you should study the works of these medieval "primitives."

Again we had to coin a phrase which may lead to all sorts of misunderstanding unless you know definitely what we mean by that word. It is derived from the Latin *primus* or "first." Therefore there have been many sorts of primitive art. There is a primitive art of the cavemen and a primitive art of the Egyptians and the Greeks, and there are American primitives. As a rule however we use the expression "primitives" to describe those pictures that were painted when the painter, after a very long absence during which he had been almost forgotten, reappeared upon the scene and when he was obliged to begin all over again and learn his trade anew. In other words, when the art of painting as we understand it today was still in its childhood.

All of us are familiar with the efforts of our own children and grandchildren when they have been given their first box of colored pencils and a few old envelopes. We cannot always quite follow them, for we don't see a cow as a square with four pegs and a pair of long horns sticking out of another square that is supposed to represent a head. Nor does a row of parallel little scratches invariably suggest an apple orchard. But to the child all these are entirely convincing and if we don't want to hurt its feelings we had better hide our own confusion and do our best to creep into the child's mind. Which is of course what we should do whenever we look at the artistic products of any bygone age. In order to understand more or less what those long-forgotten painters were trying to tell their neighbors, we must try and creep into the skins of the people who were then alive. We may never entirely succeed in this, but when we try really hard, we can do a great deal. But it takes more than good will. It takes a lot of time and patience and a vast amount of study.

As I wrote in my *ARTS*, the best thing you can hope to do, unless you have a well stocked museum near at hand, is to get a few good reproductions of those masters you want to study. Then hang them somewhere on the walls of your home where you are bound to see them constantly; keep them there and let them work in on you, as the sun worked in on the negatives of your kodak pictures, before the introduction of all those new-fangled sorts of paper which you can use with artificial light. And suddenly one day you will shout, "Now I get it! and how simple it is! Why didn't I see all this before?"

The same of course holds true for a piece of music which for a long time has meant absolutely nothing to you except a lot of meaningless noise. Hear it often enough and you may come to like it with a very sincere affection.

In all fairness, I ought to warn you that this scheme does not always work. The natural ability of the listener or the beholder has a lot to do with the eventual success. But given even a very humble amount of natural ability plus a lot of good will, you may gradually extend your power of appreciation until you may learn—if not to like—at least to respect the work of practically every old or foreign school of architecture, music, or painting.

Now while trying to understand and appreciate those primitives —while trying, for example, to make sense of a picture by Giotto— you must first of all find out in what sort of a world this man Giotto existed and what he therefore was trying to express. He lived in an age when, after a long period of spiritual hibernation, the mind of man was rewakening to all the glories and beauties of the little square of land (not yet a full-fledged globe by several centuries) on which he had to pass his two score years and five (the average age of the average man during those unhealthy and unhygienic times), while preparing himself for an infinitely happier residence in the Fields of the Blessed.

The main purpose after which all these primitives and their immediate successors were striving was one of actuality. They painted as if they were trying to tell the spectators something which they had actually seen and experienced with their own eyes. When you look at the religious works of later ages (not to mention our own times, which are pretty hopeless in that respect), you will at once notice the difference. Take the paintings and the etchings of Rembrandt, who also painted and etched a vast number of holy scenes. They are magnificently executed, but at all times you feel the "Book" that stood between the artist and his work. They are "Biblical scenes"—these paintings and etchings of Rembrandt and his contemporaries. They are illustrations of passages in the Bible. The early Italian painters did not know their Bible from reading it. They knew the sacred stories from having heard them and having lived with them until they were as much a part of their mental and spiritual make-up as the heroes of the frontier were a part of the make-up of every boy and girl of forty years ago.

Within these primitive pictures you will never come across a single stroke of doubt. Every stroke of the brush was part of that reality that was in the painter's mind and soul. He never questioned. He never had any doubts. He knew! Try as we may, we moderns all have some sort of doubts. We still may be true believers, but doubt is all around us. We cannot quite escape it. That is what makes it so difficult for us to understand both the art and the music of that particular period of the Middle Ages. The art of the questioning Greek is much closer to us than the unquestioning art of the men of the thirteenth and fourteenth centuries of our own era.

But once we have made all this clear to ourselves, an entirely new and delightful world is opened up to our astonished eyes. As I told you in the ARTS, you can learn more about the art of the latter half of the Middle Ages by reading a good life of Saint Francis of Assisi and one of Dante than by wading through a hundred hand-books on art. For then you will discover the dream world in which those people lived and worked. And since all of us, regardless of our great modernity, spend most of our time in an imaginary world of our own, it is important to understand the dreams of these Florentines and Venetians and Sienese and Paduans. Their dream centered

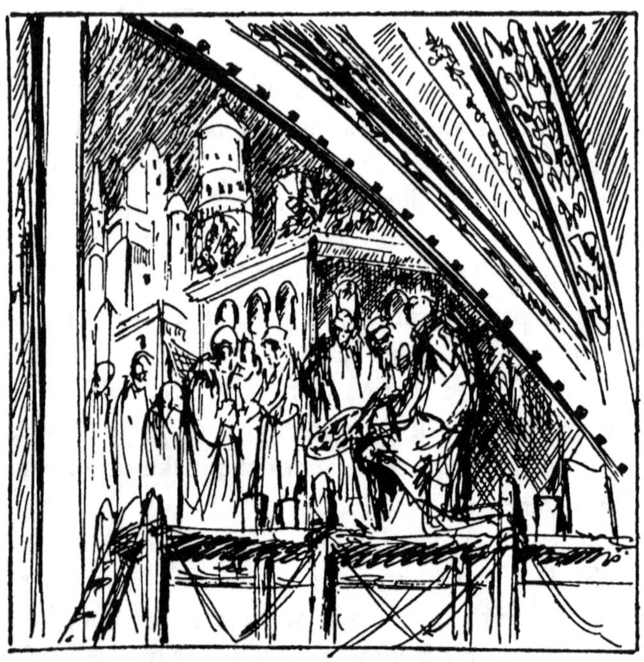

The medieval artist was merely a superior sort of craftsman without any superior "artistic notions," but he had a definite job to do and was an integral part of the community in which he lived.

around the great miracle that had come to pass in the Land of Canaan, twelve hundred years before. And they had concentrated their thoughts upon that incredible miracle until it had become the only reality in which they could take any real interest. Then they set it to paint, as Palestrina and Johann Sebastian Bach set their dreams to music, and showing it to the populace, they exclaimed, "Here is the story as we saw it, for believe it or not, we saw all this with our own eyes!"

Of course, the geographical and economic backgrounds exercised their usual influence. A worldly city like Florence, full of business and enterprise, an equally worldly city like Venice, full of adventure, luxury, and misery—these were apt to produce a different artistic atmosphere from a quiet provincial town like Siena or a Rome where everybody and everything was dominated by the presence of God's visible representative on earth. While Naples, with its hybrid population and its lazy climate and its proverbially bad government, would give birth to a sort of painters different from those of Milan, where Leonardo da Vinci might have become a really great painter if he had not spent so much of his time on the more practical pursuits of a civil engineer. But no matter where the pictures of this era were painted, they all of them have one quality in common. They speak a language of utter conviction. They tell their stories not at second hand or hearsay. The painters had been "there" in person and what they reveal unto us is something as real and actual as a modern candid photograph. And sometimes a whole lot more convincing.

"Why," so it has often been asked, "should oil painting have been invented in northern Europe when southern Europe had already been painting for centuries before northern Europe appeared upon the map?"

The answer is really very simple. All inventions are born out of necessity. In southern Europe where the Romanesque style of architecture prevailed, the painter had all the wall space he needed on which to work. In northern Europe, where Gothic had replaced the older Romanesques style, the wall space in the churches had been so greatly curtailed that murals had become almost impossible. A few illustrations showing the difference between the two sorts of construction will do more to make this clear to you than several pages of verbal explanation. The architects of France and Germany and the

Low Countries (northern Europe, to the people of the Mediterranean) had at long last solved a problem which had completely baffled both the Greeks and the Romans. They had learned how to construct a heavy roof without causing the walls of the edifice itself to collapse under this terrific burden. They had done this, not by making the walls four or five times as heavy as they used to be. For that finally would have led to complete architectural impossibilities. A church with walls twenty feet thick would have been a monstrosity. What the Gothic architects did was this. They reenforced the strength of their walls with so-called "buttresses," heavy masses of masonry which turned part of the walls into veritable (though invisible) pillars upon which the roof then came to rest. Since the walls thereupon became almost superfluous, it was possible to devote most of the wall space to those large windows which were very much needed in the rainy and dark climate of the North. These windows in turn had encouraged the work of those artists who worked in colored glass, and who now at last were given a chance to experiment with those marvelous pictures in colored (or "burned") glass which are among the most marvelous products of the medieval genius for the pictorial arts.

Meanwhile the painter had lost most of that wall space which had been his eminent domain in the older days of the Romanesque style. Since he was a painter and did not want to be deprived of his means of making a living, he began to look for some other method of practicing his craft. The walls and wet plaster were out of the question. But what could he use in their place? This puzzle was not exactly new. Even the Greeks seem to have made experiments with all sorts of mediums that could possibly be used as a base for their pigments. They had mixed their colors with vinegar and with wine and with honey and the white of eggs. And all during the earlier part of the Middle Ages this groping for the ideal base had continued, but without producing any very satisfactory results. And then, during the first quarter of the fifteenth century (Hubert van Eyck died in 1426 and Jan van Eyck died in 1441) rumor began to reach Italy that two natives of the valley of the Meuse had shown paintings done in an entirely new medium—they had mixed their colors with oil. This did not mean that after the year 1420 everybody all over the world began to paint with oil. In Italy, the artists remained faithful

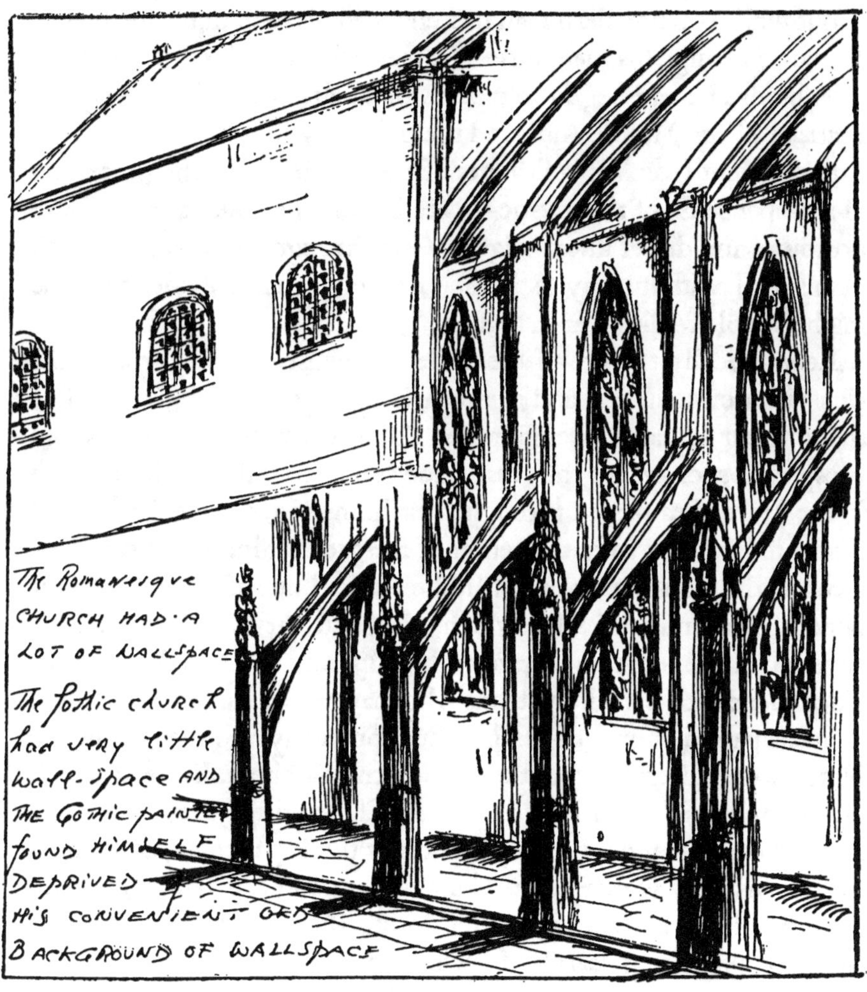

to the old fresco method for quite a long time or combined the older method with the newer one. And even today there is still some fresco work being done, especially in our own country where murals are now being painted by the square mile. But the invention (or "perfection," call it what you like) of the van Eycks completely revolutionized the art of the painter. For it set him free from his old walls. It allowed him to paint anywhere, at any time, provided he had a wooden plank or a piece of canvas to act as his background.

But while this northern man had changed his technique, he did not of course change his mentality. His mentality remained what it had been before he had begun to mix his pigments with oil. He was still a citizen of the Middle Ages and the only way in which he was perhaps different from his colleagues of the South was in the possession of a deeper sense of the mystic—a feeling that he could attain a more profound and direct knowledge of God through a systematic search of his soul without any assistance of such outside evidence as he might be able to discover in nature.

Economically the life of these Flemish artists and of those of the rich cities of southern and western Germany was very much like that of their Italian contemporaries. All of them were members of a prosperous society, for the great trade route from the Mediterranean to the North Sea passed through their home cities. And Bruges and Ghent in Flanders were the center of the greatest industrial development of the latter half of the Middle Ages. The sudden rise of that famous Burgundian duchy which, if it had survived, would have covered all the territory between the Alps and the North Sea, provided them with worldly patrons who maintained a court which was an unsurpassed center of luxury. But spiritually the men from the North were different from their southern neighbors. Being so much farther removed from the center of Christianity, they were less familiar with the more worldly aspects of the Papal court, and unlike the Italians, they were essentially an indoor people, given much more to spiritual speculations and often losing themselves completely in an uncompromising search of their immortal souls.

If you have already read a life of Saint Francis of Assisi, now try and get hold of Thomas à Kempis' *Imitation of Christ.* And when you study the early pictures of the Flemish school and the products of the German medieval school of painting, approach them from the point of view of the good Brother Thomas of Kempis, rather than from that of the son of Pietro di Bernardone. Technically during all this period between the thirteenth and fifteenth centuries, both the North and the South continued to show a steady improvement. If the North contributed the knowledge of how to paint with

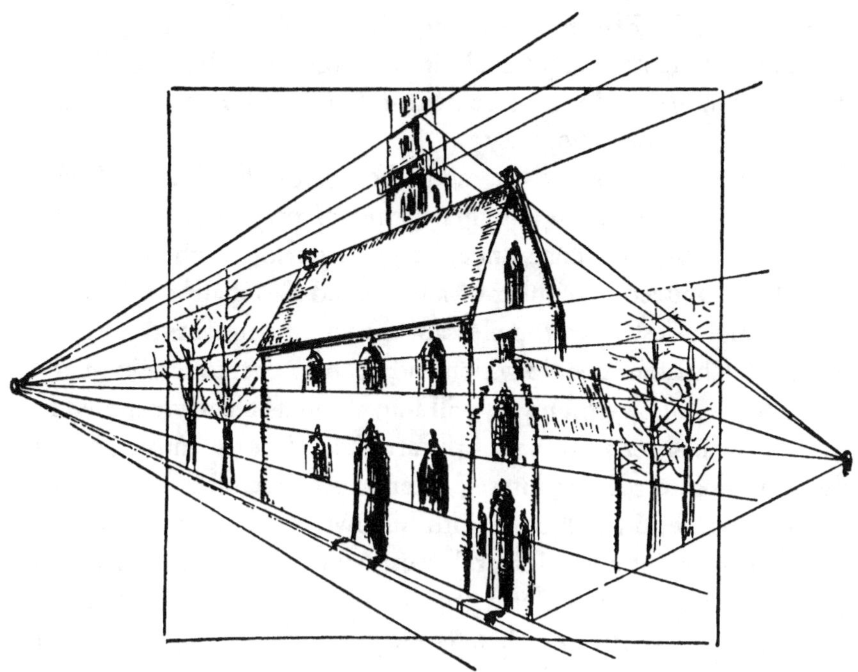

Until the end of the Middle Ages the painter had to get along as best he could without any knowledge of perspective.

oil, the South gave the world its first knowledge about that perspective without which we modern people can no longer imagine any sort of drawing or painting. And working for and in a world inspired by the same ideals, believing in the same faith and therefore still speaking a common spiritual and artistic language, they fully understood each other when they looked at each other's paintings.

It was the last time that such a condition would prevail. It was the last time that the painter could feel himself to be part of a truly universal civilization. He knew of course that there were other civilizations in other parts of the world which were different from his own. But the whole of the European continent was his field of operation. With all his little provincial idiosyncrasies, he was in the true sense of the word a citizen of the world. For in those days when it took longer to go from Bruges to Florence than it takes now to go from New York to Australia and back, it was possible to be truly internationally minded and not to be held in bondage by the prejudices of one's own race or nationality.

This feeling did not die out with the age of the Gothic. For a short time it even reached a higher degree of perfection during the Renaissance. But the Renaissance, by some curious alchemy of the spirit, also produced that spirit of a restricted nationalism which almost overnight destroyed the pleasant theory of a universal brotherhood of all Christian people which had been so characteristic of the Middle Ages. All of which you will find about as clearly exposed in the art of the painter as in that of the architect. For the musician was only beginning to reassert himself after an absence of almost twelve centuries and he did not come into his own until several hundred years after the painter and the architect. And so we should now pass over from the era of the Gothic to that of the Renaissance and try to make you see what those changes were that came over the human spirit after the middle of the fifteenth century.

GOTHIC PERIOD

ITALIAN

Giovanni Cimabue (1240–1302):
Madonna Enthroned, Lower Church, Assisi

Duccio di Buoninsegna (ca. 1260–1319):
Maestà, Cathedral Museum, Siena

Giotto di Bondone (ca. 1266–1337):
Pietà, Arena Chapel, Padua
Obsequies of St. Francis, Santa Croce, Florence
Madonna Enthroned with Angels, Uffizi, Florence

THE GOTHIC ERA

Simone Martini (ca. 1285–1344):
Annunciation, Uffizi, Florence
Christ Among the Doctors, Royal Institute, Liverpool

Pietro Lorenzetti (active 1305–1348):
Altarpiece, Santa Maria della Pieve, Arezzo

Ambrogio Lorenzetti (active 1319–1348):
Presentation in the Temple, Uffizi, Florence

Andrea Orcagna (active 1344–1368):
Altarpiece, Santa Maria Novella, Florence

Fra Angelico da Fiesole (1387–1455):
Coronation of the Virgin, San Marco, Florence
The Last Judgment, Kaiser Friedrich Museum, Berlin
Nativity, Metropolitan Museum of Art, New York

FLEMISH

Hubert van Eyck (1366–1426):
Adoration of the Lamb (completed by Jan van Eyck, St. Bavon's, Ghent)

Jan van Eyck (ca. 1380–1441):
Man with the Pinks, Kaiser Friedrich Museum, Berlin
Portrait of Jean Arnolfini and his wife, National Gallery, London

Rogier van der Weyden (ca. 1400–1464):
Descent from the Cross, Escorial, near Madrid
Annunciation, Metropolitan Museum of Art, New York

Dirck Bouts (1410–1475):
Altarpiece, St. Peter's, Louvain

Hans Memlinc (ca. 1430–1494):
Marriage of St. Catherine, St. John's Hospital, Bruges

4

THE RENAISSANCE

A new class of society has arisen and that new class has grown sufficiently rich to insist upon what it wants when it goes to the artist's studio. The painter therefore finds himself a new patron outside of the Church.

WHEN a ship bound for New York leaves Rotterdam, the passengers who come on board in the Dutch port are rather apt to look with suspicion upon those who join them in Boulogne. Thereupon the passengers from Rotterdam and Boulogne combine to accord a snooty reception to those unfortunate and misguided people who have been foolish enough to choose Southampton as their port of embarcation. As for the Irish emigrants who appear upon the scene the next afternoon at Cobh, it is beyond my power of the English language to describe the utter contempt, disdain, scorn, despisal, despiciency, despisement, vilipendency and contumely that awaits them from the side of the other passengers who have booked from Rotterdam, Boulogne, and Southampton.

A similar fate awaits the traveler along the main highway of history. Every subsequent generation looks with a deep scorn upon the achievements of its immediate predecessors, sends mamma's elegant dining room furniture to the attic (despairing of getting any money for that ridiculous rubbish), regards papa's pet novelists as hopeless, old-fashioned stick-in-the-muds and in every way endeavors to show how completely and absolutely superior it considers itself and all its ways to the manners, customs and habits of its immediate ancestors. In due course of time it may cast a sentimental backward glance upon the happy days of its great-grandparents when people went from place to place in those picturesque old stagecoaches and when the peasantry sang merry songs in beautiful rustic inns by the side of Robert Schumann's *Mühlenrad*. But the period immediately preceding has never produced anything good, has never thought a noble thought and is always altogether ridiculous. Hence such charming terms as Dark Ages and Middle Ages, as if they had been an era of no particular consequence, an inconsequential gap between the age of the Classics and the time when the spirit of the Classics was reborn in all its former glory, the so-called age of the Renaissance, the supposed rebirth of civilization.

As we are very apt to accept historical periods (like people) at their own estimate, the Renaissance in the eyes of the world at large has never lost its fine flavor as a magnificent and perpetual sort of pageant in which women with Titanesque figures strode in stately fashion from one Palladian palace to the next, listening to irresistible tunes of sweet-toned viols and occasionally helping themselves to a pinch of salt from a priceless saltcellar, wrought by the clever, if murderous hand of Benvenuto Cellini. All of which is full of glamor and therefore most welcome in a somewhat drab and monotonous world. But historically speaking, this picture is slightly out of perspective. After the days of Paolo Uccello (1397–1475), to paint entirely without perspective was no longer accepted as being quite good taste, and so we had better refrain from any further rhetoric.

For what really was the Renaissance? It was primarily a literary movement. There were other changes—changes in people's ways of thinking and in their ways of living and eating and drinking and painting and making love and music. But all these were subsidiary to the main interest of the people of the Renaissance which was in the first place a literary one.

I use the word "people" of course in a sense that might be slightly misleading if we should think of it as Abraham Lincoln did—as the whole of the populace. The "people," as we know it today, is an invention of very recent origin. The "people" of the fifteenth century were some 5 percent of the total population—the top stratum—those who were rich enough not to share the communal comb (chained to the town pump), but who could afford a comb of their own, and those who were not obliged to live twelve in a room, which served as their common parlor, dining room, kitchen and sleeping quarters. It was already quite a step forward that such a class, enjoying the rudiments of a civilized form of living, had once more arisen, and as a "civilization carrier"—to borrow an expression from the medical laboratory—it proved of the greatest possible benefit to all of us. For the middle class has always felt a profound respect for "learning." The feudal nobility that had ruled the world for the last six hundred years despised the brain. It left reading and writing and arithmetic to the few clerics it was obliged to employ as secretaries and bookkeepers. The peasants—but little removed from those domestic animals with which they shared their houses—had no need for those superfluous frills which were said to be practiced in the cities and therefore suspected as being of diabolical origin. The middle class felt differently. It had long since learned that intelligence paid and that a single chemical formula (such as that needed for the manufacture of gun-powder) was worth ten castles and ten thousand knights in armor. And it went after "Learning" with a capital L in a most serious fashion, to the great benefit of those scholars who ever since the disappearance of the old Roman civilization had been forced to live on a diet of air and an occasional dish of dried fish.

Now these native scholars, reenforced by a constantly increasing number of refugees from Constantinople (who had read the handwriting on the walls of Saint Sophia and who had decided to go while the going was still good, like the unfortunate Austrians of today), knew that Italy was still full of manuscripts which had survived from the earliest part of the Middle Ages, when the old classical tradition had not yet been completely eradicated. In the attics of churches and castles and houses and in the libraries of monasteries, there reposed an entire and complete civilization (*belles-lettres*, mathematics, physics, philosophy—everything from arithmetic to zoology) in worm-eaten manuscripts that quite often were direct copies of the Roman or Greek originals. But since nobody until then had felt the need of such enlightenment, all this material had lain there as neglected and unused as a tract on Professor Einstein's

Theory of Relativity, washed up on the shore of a remote Pacific Ocean island.

The middle class recognized the value of this buried literature as an arsenal that would provide it with all the weapons it would need in the coming and inevitable conflict with its feudal masters. Hence, for the first time since the last of the great Greek philosophers had been murdered by the mob of Alexandria and the last of the great Roman mathematicians had starved to death in some remote village in Apulia, the scholar once more became a useful and therefore honored member of society.

The demand for a cheaper method of reproduction than that afforded by the clumsy human hand had already led up to the invention of the printing press. Together the scholar and his publisher now started forth upon a mighty campaign to set the world free from ignorance and to make society safe for those who could actually read and write.

I should here stress the point that science was not exactly the strongest point of this great classical revival. Science, then as now, was still deeply feared by those who realized what one bright and courageous fellow with a lever and some elementary knowledge of physics could do toward lifting this world out of the sluggish marches of despair and indifference into which it had sunk when the last of the Greek universities had been converted into a stable or a Christian chapel. And science therefore had to overcome a great many more prejudices than literature. But the newly revealed treasure house of literature was found to be so well stocked with forgotten tomes and forgotten authors that it took centuries before all of them had been neatly catalogued, edited and placed at the disposal of the community at large.

Those centuries—or rather, that century and a half between 1400 and 1550—were the era of the true Renaissance. They were a time when the world was still inhabited by faithful children of the Church. But with a difference. The lovely fable of the Middle Ages still provided the main theme for all forms of artistic inspiration and expression. But it was quite unavoidable that certain worldly and pagan elements would almost unconsciously become incorporated into those paintings that were now being ordered by these new patrons who derived their wealth from commerce and manufacturing and not from the ownership of land or a high clerical position.

The paintings of this era therefore show an entirely novel approach to the old subject. The apostles are still the apostles of a medieval painting but now they argue and dispute with all the seriousness of Greek philosophers debating some delicate ethical problem with old Socrates. The Garden of Gethsemane begins to bear a very close resemblance to the olive tree orchard in which Plato conducted his classes in rhetoric. The audience too, which until then had played so humble a part in all these holy images, underwent a very noticeable change. It ceased to be background together with the trees and the animals of the fields. It became foreground and took a visible delight in making itself rather conspicuous. The dark and somber garments of the early days of the Middle Ages, smacking of the cloister and the nunnery, were replaced by the brilliant and colorful costumes of a class of people who not only had plenty of money but were eager to spend it on luxurious display.

In short, the whole world was being converted into one vast pageant, and private citizens (with well filled purses) now enacted the roles formerly reserved for the mighty ones of this earth and the even mightier ones of Heaven.

The art of the Renaissance therefore is much easier for us to understand than that of the Middle Ages. The Florence of the fifteenth and sixteenth centuries was the New York of today, terribly alive, very excitable, very unruly and much given to violence and crime, but also able to go to the other extreme at a moment's notice and to repent of its sins, willing to try everything once and a good many things twice, hysterical in its enthusiasms and with a profound respect for wealth and the outward and visible signs of a successful career. But fortunately the fifteenth century still felt a sense of awe before the labors of the artist. The artist, in the eyes of most people, was some sort of wizard, a divinely inspired magician, and as a result of this feeling the artist was given a free hand. He was the man to decide what was good taste and what was not. And nobody was to question his decision—at least not very much.

I should state here that such an attitude is also making itself more and more noticeable in the America of today. Our architects and painters and musicians are enjoying a much greater degree of freedom than they used to have thirty or even twenty years ago. And the results are making themselves felt in every possible way, to the immense benefit of our towns, which are becoming infinitely gayer and more harmonious than they have ever been before.

As for the Renaissance cities of Italy and Germany, you have got to see them to appreciate what a delightful sort of communal background the architects can provide if left to their own devices. And the same holds true of the pictures of that time. They reflect luxury and splendor, but it is a substantial luxury and a well moderated splendor. They also show how under the influence of the new literary enlightenment that was rapidly penetrating into every nook and corner of the old continent, the rather restricted spirit of the Middle Ages was being replaced by a much more worldly and normal point of view. Man was once more beginning to take stock of the world around him. He was still convinced that his few years on this planet were merely a preparation for everlasting happiness (or the exact opposite) in a very real hereafter. But in anticipation of that happy day when he would be set free from the miseries of his terrestrial residence, he intended to make his short sojourn on this planet as pleasant and delightful as possible. And that, I think, is the chief difference you will be able to observe in the pictures of the Gothic period and those of the age of the Renaissance.

During the earlier part of the Middle Ages, even the mighty potentate insisted that he be depicted as a saint. Now the saint no longer minded if he himself were represented with a little of the elegance of a mighty potentate or a rich merchant.

He was just as much a saint as ever. But he wanted to be part of the pageantry of life which was the chief and outstanding characteristic of that period in history when people lived in the happy illusion that they had just witnessed the rebirth of civilization.

RENAISSANCE PERIOD

ITALIAN

Paolo Uccello (1397–1475):
Battle of San Romano, National Gallery, London

Masaccio (1401–1428):
The Tribute Money, Brancacci Chapel, Carmine, Florence
Expulsion from Eden, Brancacci Chapel, Carmine, Florence

Fra Filippo Lippi (1406–1469):
Madonna and Child with Two Angels, Uffizi, Florence
Coronation of the Virgin, Uffizi, Florence
Madonna, Bache Collection, Florence

Piero della Francesca (ca. 1416–1492):
Portraits of Federigo da Montefeltro and wife, Uffizi, Florence
Resurrection, Borgo San Sepolcro

Benozzo Gozzoli (1420–1497):
Procession of the Magi, Palazzo Riccardi, Florence

Andrea del Castagno (1423–1457):
Equestrian Portrait of Niccolò da Tolentino, Duomo, Florence

Antonio Pollaiuolo (1429–1498):
Apollo and Daphne, National Gallery, London

Gentile Bellini (1429–1507):
St. Mark Preaching at Alexandria, Brera, Milan
Portrait of Doge Andrea Vendramin, Frick Collection, New York

Antonello da Messina (1430–1479):
Young Man, Metropolitan Museum of Art, New York

Carlo Crivelli (1430–1495):
Altarpiece, National Gallery, London
Madonna of the Pear Tree, Bache Collection, New York

Cosimo Tura (ca. 1430–1495):
Flight into Egypt, Bache Collection, New York

Giovanni Bellini (ca. 1430–1516):
Madonna and Saints, Frari, Venice
Allegory of the Tree of Life, Uffizi, Florence
St. Francis Receiving the Stigmata, Frick Collection, New York

Andrea Mantegna (1431–1506):
Triptych, Uffizi, Florence

Gonzaga family, Castello, Mantua
The Madonna of Victory, Louvre, Paris

Andrea Verrocchio (1435–1488):
Madonna and Two Angels, National Gallery, London

Luca Signorelli (1441–1523):
The School of Pan, Kaiser Friedrich Museum, Berlin

Sandro Botticelli (1444–1510):
The Birth of Venus, Uffizi, Florence
Primavera, Uffizi, Florence
Calumny (after Apelles), Uffizi, Florence
Magnificat, Uffizi, Florence

Pietro Perugino (1445–1523):
Crucifixion, Uffizi, Florence
The Marriage of Mary and Joseph, Art Gallery, Caen

Domenico Ghirlandaio (1449–1494):
Adoration of the Shepherds, Uffizi, Florence
Portrait of Giovanna Tornabuoni, Morgan Library, New York

Leonardo da Vinci (1452–1519):
The Last Supper, Santa Maria delle Grazie, Milan
Mona Lisa, Louvre, Paris
Madonna with St. Anne, Burlington House, London

Pintoricchio (1454–1513):
Portrait of Alexander VI, Borgia Apartments, Vatican, Rome

Vittore Carpaccio (ca. 1455–1526):
Legend of St. Ursula (nine scenes), Academy, Venice

Ambrogio da Predis (active 1472–1506):
Profile of young woman, Ambrosiana, Milan

Bernardino Luini (ca. 1475–1532):
Madonna, Louvre, Paris
Virgin and Child, Brera, Milan

Michelangelo Buonarroti (1475–1564):
The Last Judgment, Sistine Chapel, Vatican, Rome
Ceiling frescoes, Sistine Chapel, Vatican, Rome
Holy Family, Uffizi, Florence

Titian (1477–1576):
Assumption of the Virgin, Frari, Venice
Bacchus and Ariadne, National Gallery, London

Entombment, Prado, Madrid
Portrait of Aretino, Frick Collection, New York
Giorgione (1478–1510):
Fête champêtre, Louvre, Paris
Madonna Enthroned, Castelfranco del Veneto
Gypsy and Soldier, Palazzo Giovanelli, Venice
Raphael (1483–1520):
Sistine Madonna, Dresden Gallery
The Transfiguration, Vatican, Rome
Portrait of Leo X and Cardinals Rossi and Dei Medici, Pitti, Florence
Portrait of Giuliano dei Medici, Bache Collection, New York
Andrea del Sarto (1486–1531):
Madonna of the Harpies, Uffizi, Florence
Correggio (1494–1534):
La Notte, Dresden
Assumption of the Virgin, Cathedral, Parma
Danaë, Borghese Gallery, Rome
Paris Bordone (1500–1571):
Fisherman and Doge, Academy, Venice
Bronzino (1502–1572):
Youth with Book, Metropolitan Museum of Art, New York
Daniele da Volterra (1509–1566):
The Descent from the Cross, Trinità di Monti, Rome
Tintoretto (1518–1594):
Finding of St. Mark's Body, Brera, Milan
Origin of the Milky Way, National Gallery, London
Presentation in the Temple, Santa Maria dell' Orto, Venice
Giovanni Battista Moroni (ca. 1525–1578):
The Tailor, National Gallery, London
Paolo Veronese (1528–1588):
The Supper at Emmaus, Dresden Gallery
The Marriage Feast at Cana, Louvre, Paris
The Rape of Europa, Doge's Palace, Venice
Guido Reni (1575–1642):
Phoebus and Aurora, Casino of the Palazzo Rospigliosi, Rome

FLEMISH AND DUTCH

Pieter Breughel the Elder (ca. 1525–1569):
Harvesters, Metropolitan Museum of Art, New York
Winter Landscape, Hofgalerie, Vienna

Gerard David (ca. 1450–1523):
The Marriage of St. Catherine, National Gallery, London

Hieronymus Bosch (1462–1516):
Adoration of the Magi, Princeton University

Quentin Matsys (ca. 1466–1530):
The Entombment, Museum of Fine Arts, Antwerp

Jan de Mabuse (ca. 1470–1541):
Adoration of the Kings, National Gallery, London

Lucas van Leyden (ca. 1494–1533):
The Chess Players, Kaiser Friedrich Museum, Berlin

FRENCH

Jean Fouquet (ca. 1415–1480):
Portrait of Charles VII of France, Louvre, Paris
François Clouet (ca. 1510–1572):
Portrait of Elizabeth of Valois, Louvre, Paris

GERMAN

Martin Schongauer (ca. 1445–1491):
Madonna of the Rose Arbor, Colmar

Albrecht Dürer (1471–1528):
Adam and Eve, Prado, Madrid
Self-portrait, Prado, Madrid
The Adoration of the Magi, Uffizi, Florence
The Feast of Rose Garlands, Strahow monastery, near Prague

Lucas Cranach (1472–1553):
The Judgment of Paris, Karlsruhe
Portrait of John of Saxony, Dresden Gallery

Mathias Grünewald (ca. 1480–1530):
Isenheim altarpiece, Colmar

Hans Holbein the Younger (1497–1543):
Madonna of the Meyer Family, Schlossgalerie, Darmstadt
Portrait of Erasmus, Longford Castle, England
Portrait of Bonifacius Amerbach, Art Gallery, Basle

5

THE AGE OF THE BAROQUE

1600–1700

The age during which art was used to make the world once more safe for revealed and established authority.

THERE are many people nowadays who talk vaguely about rhythm. It is not easy to find out exactly what they mean, for no great exponent of the new rhythmical philosophy has as yet arisen. But I think that I know more or less what they mean. They see this world (and therefore man's mind) as being in a constant state of flux. They realize that nothing is definitely fixed, that even the remotest stars, which to the untrained eye are completely static, are forever hastening from one part of the universe to another. They observe the tides, the seasons, night following day and day following night and they are trying to discover some definite laws that cause this everlasting and regular movement from molecules to mountains.

The student of art can follow such a development very clearly in the work of the great painters. During the Middle Ages, the eyes of man are fixed on those everlasting spiritual verities which occupy most of his thoughts to the almost complete exclusion of his more worldly interests. During the Renaissance he begins to lose sight of the spiritual qualities of human existence and stresses the pleasures of a normal, everyday existence, enjoying the good things of this life as part of his legitimate inheritance. He once more takes notice of the physical world around him. He travels far and wide. He visits China and he catches a glimpse of the riches of the Indies. He explores the long forgotten coasts of Africa and the outskirts of a new and hitherto unsuspected continent called America. He piles up vast fortunes from the trade in foreign spices. He plunders his distant neighbors with an unprecedented zeal. And after he has lived for centuries on such a small margin of safety that he has grown completely indifferent to his physical surroundings, contenting himself with a meagre meal in a cold and uncomfortable house, he now partakes of noble repasts, surrounded by all the luxuries which money can buy.

So far so good. But he seemed to forget that it takes all sorts of people to make this world the interesting place it is. He overlooked the fact that there are two types of human beings—those who derive immense pleasure from looking at a beautiful picture or a lovely woman and listening to delightful music in a noble hall filled with colorful tapestries and heavily carved furniture and those who obtain their only real happiness from the exact opposite and from denying themselves all those pleasures, from turning their backs upon the beautiful pictures and the lovely women and from closing their ears to the tempting tunes played so seductively in that noble hall filled with colorful tapestries and heavily carved furniture. That however seems to be part of the rhythm of this world. As a result of which every era of a great worldliness of spirit is invariably followed by another one which seeks happiness and perfection from practicing the virtues of asceticism and self-denial.

The age therefore which gave us Saint Peter's and the palaces of Italy, the expression of a serious desire to anticipate the heavenly Paradise by establishing a makeshift Paradise right here on this planet, was followed by a period during which man searched his soul more seriously than ever before. The Reformation was a concrete expression of this new spirit of unworldliness and it came so unexpectedly and with such violence that it almost destroyed the old fabric not only of the Church but also of society itself. However, an institution like the Church, so carefully reared during so many centuries, proved itself too strong to be permanently weakened by even so serious an assault. For a moment the Church reeled as if dazed by the blow. Then it gathered all its forces together and prepared for a mighty counter-attack. It began to realize that this was not merely a local revolution caused by a rebellious German monk who was too honest in his convictions to be persuaded into a compromise with his own convictions. If it were to regain all the lost territory (the greater part of northern Europe), it must proceed very carefully and very slowly and fight the battle all along the line. In order to do this, it must first of all put its own house in order and bring about a number of highly necessary reforms. Then it must devise ways and means of regaining the confidence and the good will of those who had deliberately turned their backs upon their old Mother, the Church. In this struggle it was not enough to have a mighty army of soldiers and the support of powerful princes. For a sword can kill but it cannot force an honest man to change his opinions. Other and more subtle allies must be enlisted, that all might be once more brought within the fold of the faithful. Hence the painter as well as the architect and the musician now found himself in the fortunate position of being for once desperately needed by a patron who also could pay him most liberally for his services. Hence the rise of that era which came to be known as the age of the Baroque. Michelangelo (in case you want a name to help you remember the necessary dates) was the first of the great masters of the Baroque and he died in the year 1564, almost half a century after the beginning of the Reformation. In certain parts of Europe and America (the Baroque style became very popular in the Spanish colonies in the new world), Baroque continued until the end of the eighteenth century. But its main force had spent itself around the year 1700 when it was at last beginning to be realized that the conflict between the two opposing forces (Church and Reformation) must necessarily end in a compromise. During that century and a half, however, the heavy style of the Baroque had made itself felt in every sort of architecture, music and painting. Its main characteristic was a desire to impress, to impose itself upon the beholder or the listener by the stateliness of its approach. The people of the Renaissance had also been great sticklers for form. No matter what they did, whether they took a walk or sat down to dinner or danced a minuet or entertained their guests, they had always been conscious of the fact that they were supposed to be playing a role in a most noble pageant. But it had been a decidedly worldly sort of pageant. Now the performance itself continued as before but the stage-setting was completely changed and the actors too felt compelled to speak a different sort of lines and to omit all that comedy element that had been so dear to the hearts of the contemporaries of Good Queen Bess and her most loyal subject, Master William Shakespeare of the village of Stratford-on-Avon.

You will notice this change very clearly in the pictures that have come to us from those days. But when you look at them, you must remember that another element had entered upon the scene which was responsible for the rapid spread of the so-called Baroque style. The Reformation had caused a new political development on the European continent. It had given birth to the idea of nationalism. Not in our modern sense of the word, when nationalism is usually associated with race. It didn't any more know what that word meant than I do. It was a nationalism created by a number of competing dynasties. They now had their chance. The Reformation had destroyed that old ideal of a universality of empire (both in a worldly and clerical conception of the word) which had so completely dominated the mind of medieval man. The cutting up of the map of Europe into little scraps of territory, each one with its own church and catechism, had offered ambitious rulers and statesmen an opportunity to do something which they had often enough tried to do during the Middle Ages but in which they had never been entirely successful. They were now, each within his own bailiwick, straining every nerve to create as highly centralized a kingdom or duchy as they could possibly hope to do before their jealous neighbors should grow sufficiently powerful to interfere with their own ambitions. It was only natural that in southern Europe, where the people had remained faithful to the old faith, the Church and the monarchy should make common cause and should combine forces in their warfare upon the heretic and the rebel. Especially in Spain which had made itself the worldly champion of the Church, this spirit of the Baroque made itself evident in the paintings of the contemporary masters, who concentrated their efforts upon a very successful attempt to glorify both the Church and that dynasty which ruined itself in its whole-hearted but costly effort to maintain the *status quo* of two centuries before.

But the paintings of the seventeenth century clearly show how closely art is connected with life and how accurately it reflects the spirit of the times that gave it birth. The Low Countries had borne the main burden of the struggle on the part of the Protestant nations of northern Europe. After a terrific fight they had finally set themselves free from the domination of Spain. Their architecture was therefore hardly affected by the Baroque. They went directly from the style of the Renaissance to that of the Rococo and skipped the Baroque. But their painting shows even more clearly how completely they had set themselves free from the older traditions. Technically they were the successors of the medieval Flemish painters who had established the Flemish school of the Gothic period but now they set their technical virtuosity to work upon an entirely new sort of subjects, very simple, everyday subjects that would appeal to the tastes and the rather limited pocketbooks of that class of society which formerly would never have dreamed of buying pictures for the embellishment of their own homes—the commercial middle class, which until then would never have thought of making such an investment.

Their German neighbors fared less well. The Thirty Years War (that prolonged religious struggle that lasted from 1618 until 1648) had so completely ruined the medieval prosperity of that country that there was no extra money for any of the arts, least of all that of the painter. England was only slowly emerging from the Middle Ages and generally speaking has always been too much interested in other forms of art to devote much of her genius to painting. France was too busy with her internal process of dynastic centralization to be ready yet for a revival of the pictorial arts. And generally speaking, with the exception of the Low Countries and Spain, painting was not one of the most outstanding forms of art of the Baroque period. It was too restless a time—life was too full of violence and the fury of war and persecution to allow the painter that peace of mind which he needs to be able to do his best work. He found it again in the age of the Rococo when once more, and perhaps for the last time, Europe enjoyed something that vaguely resembled a common civilization.

BAROQUE PERIOD

DUTCH AND FLEMISH

Peter Paul Rubens (1577–1640):
- *The Descent from the Cross*, Cathedral, Antwerp
- *Chapeau de paille*, National Gallery, London
- *The Three Graces*, Prado, Madrid
- Portrait of Isabella Brant, Old Pinakothek, Munich

Frans Hals (ca. 1580–1666):
- *Laughing Cavalier*, Wallace Collection, London
- *The Merry Company*, Metropolitan Museum of Art, New York

Sir Anthony Van Dyck (1599–1641):
- *St. Martin Dividing his Cloak*, National Gallery, London
- Portrait of James Stuart, Duke of Lennox, Metropolitan Museum of Art, New York
- Portrait of Maria Luisa von Tassis, Liechtenstein Gallery, Vienna

Rembrandt Harmenzoon van Rijn (1606–1669):
- *The Night Watch*, Rijks Museum, Amsterdam
- *The Anatomy Lesson*, Mauritshuis, The Hague
- *Christ at Emmaus*, Louvre, Paris
- Portrait of Hendrickje Stoffels, Metropolitan Museum of Art, New York

Gerard Dou (1613–1675):
- *The Dropsical Woman*, Louvre, Paris

Gerard Ter Borch (1617–1681):
- *The Peace of Münster*, National Gallery, London
- *Woman Pouring Wine*, Metropolitan Museum of Art, New York

Philip Wouwerman (1619–1668):
- *The Halt*, Metropolitan Museum of Art, New York

Aelbert Cuyp (1620–1691):
- *Riders with Boy and Herdsman*, National Gallery, London
- *Landscape with Cattle*, Metropolitan Museum of Art, New York

Paul Potter (1625–1654):
- *The Young Bull*, Mauritshuis, The Hague

Jan Steen (1626–1679):
Village Doctor, Brooklyn Museum
The Prince's Birthday, Rijks Museum, Amsterdam

Jacob van Ruysdael (ca. 1628–1682):
Landscape with Ruins, National Gallery, London
The Mountain Torrent, Metropolitan Museum of Art, New York

Pieter de Hooch (ca. 1629–1677):
The Visit, Metropolitan Museum of Art, New York

Jan Vermeer (1632–1675):
A Letter, Rijks Museum, Amsterdam
View of Delft, Mauritshuis, The Hague
Sleeping Girl, Metropolitan Museum of Art, New York

Nicolaas Maes (1632–1693):
The Cradle, National Gallery, London
Saying Grace, Louvre, Paris

Meindert Hobbema (1638–1709):
The Avenue, Middelharnis, National Gallery, London

AMERICAN

John Singleton Copley (1737–1815):
The Death of Chatham, National Gallery, London
Portrait of John Hancock, Museum of Fine Arts, Boston

Gilbert Stuart (1755–1828):
"Athenaeum" Portrait of George Washington, Museum of Fine Arts, Boston
"Landsdowne" portrait of Washington, Pennsylvania Academy of Fine Arts, Philadelphia

ENGLISH

Sir Peter Lely (1618–1680):
Series of portraits of court beauties, Hampton Court Palace, near London
Portrait of the Duchess of Cleveland, Metropolitan Museum of Art, New York

Sir Godfrey Kneller (1646–1723):
Portrait of Lady Mary Berkeley, Metropolitan Museum of Art, New York

William Hogarth (1697–1764):
- Self-portrait, National Gallery, London
- *The Shrimp Girl*, National Gallery, London

Sir Joshua Reynolds (1723–1792):
- *The Age of Innocence*, National Gallery, London
- *Mrs. Siddons as the Tragic Muse*, Huntington Gallery, San Marino, California

Thomas Gainsborough (1727–1788):
- *The Blue Boy*, Huntington Gallery, San Marino, California
- Portrait of Mrs. Siddons, National Gallery, London

George Romney (1734–1802):
- *Lady Hamilton as a Bacchante*, National Gallery, London
- *The Gower Children*, National Gallery, London

Sir Henry Raeburn (1756–1823):
- Self-portrait, National Gallery, Edinburgh

Sir Thomas Lawrence (1769–1830):
- *Nature*, Metropolitan Museum of Art, New York
- *Pinkie*, Huntington Gallery, San Marino, California

FRENCH

Nicolas Poussin (1594–1665):
- *The Blind Orion*, Metropolitan Museum of Art, New York
- *Venus Surprised*, National Gallery, London
- *Triumphs of Flora*, Louvre, Paris

Claude Lorrain (1600–1682):
- Landscape, Metropolitan Museum of Art, New York

ITALIAN

Annibale Carracci (1560–1609):
- Frescoes in the Palazzo Farnese, Rome

Michelangelo Amerighi da Caravaggio (1569–1609):
- *The Card Players*, Palazzo Sciarra, Rome
- Portrait of a Knight of Malta, Louvre, Paris
- *The Supper at Emmaus*, National Gallery, London

Luca Giordano (1632–1705):
- *The Story of Judith*, San Martino, Naples

Giovanni Battista Tiepolo (1696–1770):

Holy Family, Academy, Venice

St. Catherine of Siena, Imperial Gallery, Vienna

SPANISH

Domenico Theotocopuli, known as El Greco (ca. 1548–1614):

The Burial of Count Orgaz, St. Tomé, Toledo

St. Maurice and the Theban Legion, Escorial, Madrid

View of Toledo, Metropolitan Museum of Art, New York

Portrait of Cardinal de Guevara, Metropolitan Museum of Art, New York

Francisco de Zurbarán (1586–1662):

Apotheosis of St. Thomas Aquinas, Provincial Museum, Seville

José Ribera (1588–1656):

Pietà, National Gallery, London

Mary Magdalen, Prado, Madrid

Diego Rodríguez de Silva y Velázquez (1599–1660):

Portrait of Marianna of Austria, Prado, Madrid

Los Borrachos, Prado, Madrid

The Surrender of Breda, Prado, Madrid

Las Meninas, Prado, Madrid

Bartolomé Esteban Murillo (1617–1682):

The Immaculate Conception, Louvre, Paris

St. Thomas of Villanueva Distributing Alms, Provincial Museum, Seville

Francisco José de Goya y Lucientes (1746–1828):

Portrait of Don Manuel Osorio de Zuñiga, Bache Collection, New York

Family of Charles IV, Prado, Madrid

The Bullfight, Metropolitan Museum of Art, New York

6

THE AGE OF THE ROCOCO

1600–1700

The great age of charm and elegance is most carefully reflected by the painter.

THE era of the Rococo, like that of the Middle Ages, was dominated by a beautiful dream and in quite the same way it was rudely awakened from its pleasant phantasies by a terrible disaster. In the case of the Middle Ages, that disaster was called the Reformation. In the case of the age of the Rococo, that brutal reality is known to us as the Great French Revolution. This is not meant as a reflection upon either the Reformation or the Revolution. Both of them were inevitable events in the chain of circumstances that is slowly bringing mankind to that higher degree of personal and spiritual liberty which we hold to be the ultimate purpose of all true progress. (*I am writing this March* 14, 1938. *For the moment I have my doubts. H. v. L.*)

Fortunately for the artist, he is neither a politician nor a conscious propagandist. Being a citizen of his own day and age, it is merely his duty to represent the spirit of his own time in stone, in paint or in sound. When he has done this to the best of his honest ability, he has done his job and that is all we can ask of him. It is therefore not fair to hold it up against many of the men of the Rococo period because they paid so little respect to the seamy side of life. They knew that it existed but they happened to live at a time when society felt sincerely convinced that it was on the point of solving most of its age-old problems by the introduction of an entirely new principle—a principle that insisted upon the application of reason to all the problems of every-day life. Of course, what they exactly meant by that word "reason," they never bothered to explain, or, whenever they did so, they so completely lost themselves in a luscious jungle of high-sounding phrases that they were apt to obscure the issue until nobody knew what they were talking about. The same, however, has held true for every other historical period that was dominated by some convenient and resplendent slogan. Liberty, Fraternity, Equality—Democracy—Faith—Heil Hitler—Proletarians of all Countries Unite!—Our Lives for the Czar!—the air has always been full of them and having, for a short while, acted as a convenient battle-cry for this or that or the other cause, they are thereupon sent to the Museum of Historical Curiosities, together with the arquebuses and the mail and chain coats and the Paisley shawls of our grandfathers and great-grandfathers.

The artist, however, has a somewhat different duty from the ordinary citizen. He does not work for the moment. He must discover and reveal those elements of lasting value that lie hidden in every human soul and in every human relationship and in every bit of scenery. And his greatness—or lack thereof—depends upon his ability to detect and depict those elements in such a way that they shall be clear and evident not only to his contemporaries but also to the people of an entirely different age.

Let me try to make this clear by giving you an example. Giotto and the Italian primitives lived in a world with which we no longer have a single contact. Their pictures, however, do make sense. They fascinate us by the simplicity of their appeal and it is a pleasure to have a good reproduction on our walls. The last of the Hapsburgs lost his throne long ago. The pictures that were painted for their benefit lie rolled up in the cellars of the Prado, to escape destruction by the guns of General Franco. The philosophy of life and the theory of government of these men, who only a few centuries ago ruled half of the world (civilized and otherwise), are merely interesting to the student of human stupidity. But Velásquez speaks a language we still understand very well. The Flanders of Brueghel and the Holland of Rembrandt no longer exist, but their work remains as fresh as if it had been painted only yesterday. The great Chinese masters wrought in a medium that is completely foreign to us, yet we take great delight in their black and white landscapes. And so it goes. What is genuine in a work of art can never be destroyed. For it represents something basic, something essential, and therefore, like a great truth, it is bound to neither time nor place. The people of the Rococo do not enjoy a very good place in our age,

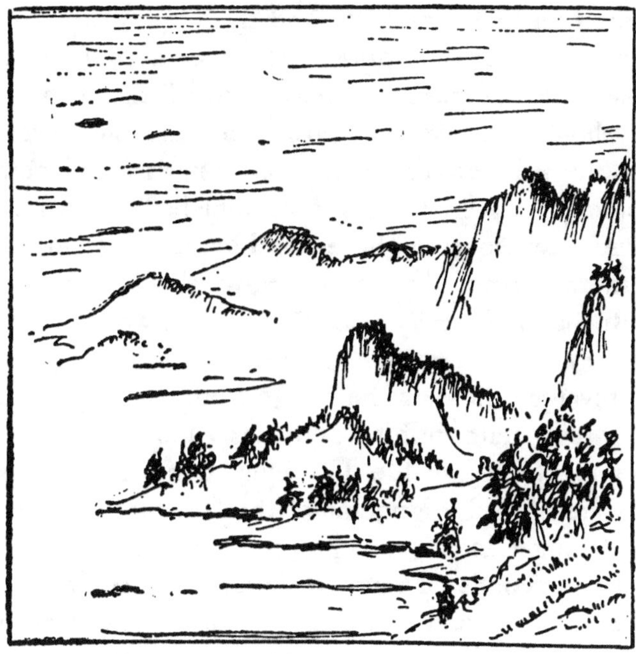

The art of China is at first a closed book to us because it was chiefly an art of "suggestion" and avoided all photographic accuracy.

which has reduced everything to a few economic principles. We accuse them of having been wasteful in the extreme and completely indifferent to the suffering of the lower classes. The first of these two statements is undoubtedly correct. They were great lovers of luxury, although it should be said in their defence that they knew how to live luxuriously with genuine elegance and with an almost touching kind of simplicity. The second one is based on prejudice rather than on fact. It is only very slowly that we are beginning to get the right perspective upon this century in which idealism was so strongly blended with many and inexcusable remnants of the Middle Ages and the era of the Baroque. Dickens' *Tale of Two Cities* is still the source from which most people get their notion about the period just preceding the French Revolution. And the wasteful rule of King Louis XIV seemed a very appropriate introduction to that age when a French Queen was supposed to have said that if the people had no bread, they should eat cake. We now know that she never made that remark. She had heard of a lack of bread in Paris and merely inquired whether there were not any rolls to be had either. I mention this otherwise inconsequential little detail because it seems as if we shall need another hundred years before we shall begin to see the era of the Rococo as it really was. Perhaps the worst we can say about it is this: that it was an age of sentimentalism. And this sentimentalism prevented those on the bridge from seeing whither they were steering their craft until it was too late, and they ran it on the rocks with a terrific loss of life. However, until the very last moment they were blissfully ignorant of the fate that awaited them. They knew (being as intelligent a group of men and women as ever existed) that all was not well in the steerage and the second class, but now that they were learning to set their compass by the brilliant star of Pure Reason, something would soon be done about this unfortunate state of affairs and they would get their craft safely into port. In the meantime it would be foolish not to enjoy the pleasant quarters on the main deck and make life on board as pleasant as possible.

You will find this spirit very clearly reflected in the art of this period. It is most conspicuously present in the buildings erected during the eighteenth century. It is one of the main characteristics of the music of that period. And the painters too show how they worked for a market that stressed the idea of charm at the cost of almost everything else. One could be poor or rich, one could be sick or in radiant health, one could be young or old, one could be saint or sinner, but one must remember to die gracefully, to suffer charmingly, or to be successful and famous with a becoming degree of elegance. Hence there is a certain uniformity about the art of this era. In the end one begins to feel as a man must feel who has been married for quite a long time to a woman who makes a profession of being charming. And the art of this era lacks that sense of virility and strength which is such an agreeable quality of the art of the Renaissance and the Baroque. It is a woman's art, rather than a man's, but then it was a woman's age rather than a man's age, as you will notice from the clothes worn by the men and the furniture on which they were supposed to sit and drink polite chocolate out of lovely cups of china while engaged in a polite bit of gossip.

All this is true and except from certain technical angles, this was quite surely not the greatest art that was ever painted. It deserves however our very careful attention for it was the last time in history that the artist had an opportunity to depict a society and a civilization that was truly an international society and civilization and not in any sense a national one. During the age of the Baroque, the highly centralized dynastic state had made its appearance and the nobility had lost a great deal of its former political and economic importance. It had however survived as a most convenient and useful social background for the actual occupants of the throne, who often enough, I am afraid, felt a bit awkward amidst the splendor of their recently acquired palaces.

During the age of the Rococo their Majesties had gradually overcome their original shyness, and for lack of suitable candidates they, as well as their noble attendants, had usually married into the few hundred families provided with sufficiently long pedigrees to qualify as breeders of a blue-blooded offspring. It was this very clannishness which contributed so greatly to the establishment of that cosmopolitan society which I mentioned a moment ago. Whether they lived in the heart of Russia or in Sweden near the Polar Circle or on the windswept plateau of Castile or on some rocky promontory of the Dalmatian coast, whether they were Protestants, Catholics or believed in nothing at all—all these well-bred people had certain ideas in common, or perhaps it would be better to say certain modes of behavior which in turn presupposed certain very definite ideas upon every subject from the rearing of children to the way one should carry one's handkerchief.

This cosmopolitan civilization, which had been quite common in the classical days of Rome, when both Paul of Tarsus and mighty Caesar had boasted of being Roman citizens—this universal outlook upon life which had been able to maintain itself during the Middle Ages while the Church was in power and which had even somehow weathered the storm of the Reformation and the Baroque, now made itself visible and audible for the last time. It may return to our world when the brotherhood of the proletariat or the *fascisti* shall at last have become a fact instead of being merely an unholy wish on the part of some of my neighbors whom I do not like. But after the Rococo it disappeared from the face of the earth. Nationalism took the place of cosmopolitanism and the painter was once more out of luck.

ROCOCO PERIOD

FRENCH

Antoine Watteau (1684–1721):

Le Mezzetin, Metropolitan Museum of Art, New York

The Embarkation for Cythera, Louvre, Paris

Jean Marc Nattier (1685–1766):

Portrait of Mme. de Pompadour, Marseilles Museum

Portrait of Louise Henriette de Bourbon, Versailles

Princesse de Condé as Diana, Metropolitan Museum of Art, New York

Nicolas Lancret (1690–1743):

The Music Lesson, Louvre, Paris

Jean Baptiste Chardin (1699–1779):

The Benediction, Louvre, Paris

Self-portrait, Louvre, Paris

Young Woman Knitting, Metropolitan Museum of Art, New York

François Boucher (1703–1770):

Toilet of Venus, Metropolitan Museum of Art, New York

Rinaldo and Armida, Louvre, Paris

Quentin de La Tour (1704–1788):

Portrait of Jean Jacques Rousseau, Louvre, Paris

Portrait of Mlle. Fel, St. Quentin Museum

Charles André Vanloo (1705–1765):

The Concert, Wallace Collection, London

Jean Baptiste Greuze (1725–1805):

The Broken Pitcher, Louvre, Paris

Jean Honoré Fragonard (1732–1806):

Romance of Love and Youth, Frick Collection, New York

ITALIAN

Canaletto (1697–1768):

The Piazzetta, Venice, Metropolitan Museum of Art, New York

Pietro Longhi (1702–1785):

Exhibition of Rhinoceros, National Gallery, London

Francesco Guardi (1712–1793):

Masquerade in the Ridotto, Correr Museum, Venice

7

REVOLUTION AND EMPIRE

1785–1815

The Painter Turns Propagandist

I HAVE already relieved my feelings upon the subject of the artist as a propagandist. So this chapter can be very short. The half dozen years of the French Revolution will show you in a most eloquent fashion what happens when a man's membership ticket in a definite political party is more important than his ability to handle a brush or balance his strings and his brasses. And the style that followed upon the classical simplicity of the Revolution (when every hired assassin had been a Cincinnatus and every cheap demagogue a most noble Brutus) and that was associated with Napoleon's empire, was equally banal and uninspired. I write it down because it has to be mentioned in a brief book of this sort, but that is all. The point of view of the painter during the revolutionary era was either one of immense enthusiasm or it was inspired by the reflection, "How do I keep my head on my shoulders?"

As for the Empire style, it was typical of the master who had created it—a vulgar little upstart with enough energy to keep an entire continent in an uproar for almost twenty years but with the personal tastes of a speak-easy owner who has struck it rich.

You will find very little good art dating back to this period except when it was painted by very strong characters like Goya, who could keep themselves aloof from all the hocus-pocus that went on around them and destroyed the weaker brethren. But after the beginning of the nineteenth century you have to look at art with quite a different set of eyes from those you needed during the previous ten thousand years. After the beginning of the nineteenth century, the artist ceased to be a necessity. He became a luxury. And not even a very popular one.

8

THE TWENTIETH CENTURY

The painter gains his individual liberty, which was undoubtedly a great step forward for him as a "person" but which seems to have done very little good to him as an artist.

GENERALIZATIONS are always dangerous, yet in a chapter like this they are almost unavoidable. For we are now able to look back at almost a century and a half of painting. Since the disappearance of the older order of things, everything is still in quite as much of a muddle as it was fifty or seventy years ago.

Now what is the cause of this? And who is responsible? As always in history, nobody is really responsible because everybody is responsible and there is not one single cause but there are dozens of causes, each one contributing its own little mite in its own way and adding to the general confusion of ideas which has been so characteristic of the painter's art during the whole of the nineteenth century, and which has continued during the past thirty-eight years of the twentieth.

What I am going to give you is a very personal view of the situation and I don't pretend that it is the only true solution of the problem, but at least it is a concrete attempt at reaching some sort of a solution.

The great Revolution had definitely done away with the worship of birth and rank. It had immediately established a new worm of worship of its own—the worship of money. Whereas formerly anything could be done by those who had inherited a title, now everything was within the reach of those who had accumulated a sufficiently large number of ducats. This change had already made itself noticeable during the days of the Terror. The rich fared undoubtedly much better than the poor. Robespierre had not for nothing been given the name of the "Incorruptible." He was indeed as incorruptible as Adolf Hitler. But the fact that he could not be "reached" was sufficiently rare to attract the immediate attention of the public at large.

Napoleon had the middle class Italian's respect for wealth. And when he disappeared, the industrial revolution was beginning to make itself felt. Thereafter money became the chief criterion by which a man's success in life was measured.

It is quite true, as was once said by a clever historian, that aristocracy means old money. But like old wine, the old money had acquired certain qualities which made it more palatable than the vintage of the year before last. For aristocracy was wise enough to know that it could not hope to survive without certain very definite standards. And art too, in the days of its greatest triumph, had accepted the existence of standards. They may have been right and they may have been wrong. In our own age, with its contempt for rigid rules, it has become very popular to denounce all standards of conduct and behavior as absurd rules of a bygone age that had better be forgotten. I am going to debate this point. Beckmesser is not an attractive figure in Richard Wagner's *Meistersinger*. But Beckmesser was an absurdity and the poetry of Hans Sachs too shows that this master was not averse to the use of definite rules of prosody. In other words, as soon as the artist ceased to be merely a craftsman of superior ability, he lost touch with the world of the guilds, which had been a world of realities, and became something that was neither fish, fowl nor good red herring. I do not mean to imply that his technical ability was less great than it had formerly been. Often it was greater than that of previous generations, just as today the technical ability of the average musician is infinitely greater than that of the virtuosi of a century ago. There are now in every American city of some size at least a dozen boys and girls who can play the Schumann concerto probably quite as well as that poor man's widow played it in the fifties of the last century. And our art schools turn out thousands of graduates who can copy Rembrandt's picture of his son

Titus almost as well as Rembrandt had painted the original. No, the technical ability is as great as ever among the best of our contemporary masters. But they fail to make their mark because they live in a sort of artistic vacuum. They undoubtedly have something to say, but what is the use of saying it when nobody cares to listen?

This brings us to our next point: what has brought about this general indifference toward the arts? Again there are quite a number of contributory influences and again it is very difficult to say which of these has been the most disastrous. Let me try and give you a few.

I have already pointed to the disappearance of the guilds and of the high standards of craftsmanship of which they had been the guardians for so many centuries. The artist therefore became a free agent and he could paint as he liked. But not entirely, for now another agency suddenly arose to control him in his activities. That was the art critic. Ever since the seventeenth century there had been people who wrote books about painters, giving short outlines of their lives and perhaps a few outstanding examples of their work, but rarely venturing so far as to offer any opinions which might be construed as criticisms in the modern sense of the word.

All that changed after the middle of the eighteenth century. A new science, or rather pseudo-science, was invented by the learned professors of Germany. It was called aesthetics and undertook to provide us with a definite theory about the true nature of beauty. Thus far people had instinctively liked certain things or had turned their backs upon them and nobody had asked them to explain why they felt that way. Might as well ask a man to tell you why he loves Gorgonzola cheese yet hates spinach or vice versa. Aesthetics were very popular among the sentimental folk of the era of the Rococo. Reason was to solve all our problems and aesthetics were to guide reason in accepting that which contained elements of true greatness and in rejecting that which was not worthy of our admiration.

It did not take very long for the aesthetically inclined philosopher to change himself into a full-fledged art critic and since even aesthetically inclined philosophers must live, they began to sell their wares to the newspapers and the periodicals, since editors were the only people who would pay them money for their labors.

When the subject of the art critic comes up among the artists (as it is apt to do after about five minutes of conversation), they all agree that the art critic is a completely superfluous individual who as a rule (from the artist's point of view) knows less than nothing about the subject upon which he is supposed to be an expert and that he is by no means worthy of their serious attention. That may be true but even the most bitter of their enemies know that painters and musicians nowadays cannot possibly hope to achieve anything without the support and the approval of these deeply despised interlopers into the Garden of the Muses, and therefore all of them have learned to cater more or less to their enemy, the critic. You can easily see how this has affected not only the painter but also the musician and the sculptor and every one even remotely engaged in an artistic pursuit. Whereas formerly the artist appealed directly to the consumer—painted his pictures and sold them to his patron or exposed them to the view of the populace in either church or palace—he must now take account of the fact that a third party has deliberately pushed himself into that narrow open space between the picture on the wall and the spectator standing in front of it and that that third party has taken it upon himself to explain the inner meaning and the technical perfections or imperfections of the canvas to a public that is no longer supposed to have any opinions of its own.

I need not waste any more words upon this subject, for every one of my readers is sure to have been exposed to the ministrations of the critic. You go to a concert and an elaborately printed program tells you in detail what the composer has meant to convey when in the first phrase of the second movement he begins with a long blast of the French horns followed by a rapid passage on the bull-fiddles. And how often have you gone to an exhibition of pictures without first having read a lot about it in your newspapers in an article signed by a duly accredited art critic? You may have been told or you may merely suspect that the fellow has no more taste than a publisher of colored picture postal cards but he is the "critic" and you are the "layman" and therefore he "knows" and you don't.

By and large I would say that the critic has done infinitely more harm than good to the cause of art. For being as a rule an artist who had too little ability of his own to make good, he now enjoys the power which the printed word gives him to lord it over his former colleagues and to give vent to his own preferences and prejudices with all the cunning and bitterness of a man who has been frustrated in his real ambitions. In order to maintain himself he must have followers and he must build up a party of his own with the same painstaking care with which a bright youngster, wishing to become a political leader, builds up the machine in his own ward. The youngster bound for the political heights knows that he has rivals who are trying to do the same thing and that a violent if artificial partisanship is a necessary part of the game. The critic, although he lives in much more rarified atmosphere than the political hoodlum, follows exactly the same method. He can make himself pleasantly conspicuous by attacking the most recent composer and by calling Franz Liszt or Richard Wagner charlatans and nit-wits and musical crooks, while his rival on the opposition paper just across the street hails them as the true prophets of a new age. He can denounce Degas or Daumier or Whistler as a crew of despicable impostors and poltroons, because he knows that the moment they try to defend themselves he can publicly expose them as weaklings, who cannot take it and who have been found guilty of that terrible offense against good sportsmanship which bids the artist grin and bear it, no matter how unfairly he has been attacked by some local critic.

For in the Europe of the last century the critic worked not infrequently in close (though secret) harmony with the art dealer and by his articles he was quite often able to create a fashionable market for the paintings which the art dealer intended to foist upon the public.

Publicity may be a useful and even necessary element in disposing of breakfast foods and cosmetics, but it has done infinite harm to the Arts. It has made a few painters and a great many art dealers rich, but it has made the Arts a subject of speculation and of sudden crazes and of those outbreaks of fashionable interest which like bonfires on ice give a marvelous light while they actually burn but which die down even more rapidly than they got started.

If from all this, you conclude that the artist's life during the nineteenth century was not a happy one, you have concluded rightly. The painters continued to exist just as the composers (even more sorely beset by outward circumstances) continued to exist. The good ones could not help themselves and so they would paint or compose regardless of everything. But unless they had a gift for salesmanship and a rather elastic conscience, they deeply felt the absurdity of their position, for they were doing something which they felt to be without any direct purpose. They were creating forms of beauty which no longer seemed to fit into the scheme of things. Here and there a private citizen might buy one of their pieces because they genuinely liked it or because it flattered their vanity to pose as a protector of the Arts or (listening to the confidential talks of their art dealer) because it promised to be a good investment. Now and then the state, thinking of the Arts as a convenient means of advertising its high cultural standards, would acquire a little canvas that was thereupon buried in a museum. But the times were gone when an entire city would grow excited about a new picture in one of its churches or when pope and king would quarrel with each other for the services of some particular artist.

The painter had gained his liberty but in so doing he had acquired the status of an artistic vagabond. In former ages he might have been poor, but he had not liked it and had worked until he got a better competence. Now he became the Bohemian, in ribald and unkempt protest against the conventions of a society that had cast him out.

Being no longer constrained in his activities by any definite standards, the artist became the great experimenter. He tried everything, not once but twice or three times. He borrowed from the Chinese and the Persians and the Aztecs and strange African tribes, and he declared himself free from all those restrictive rules of form or color which had been accepted without a murmur by the genius of a bygone age. He turned his studio into a laboratory in which he dissected light as Vesalius had dissected his stolen corpses, but less successfully. He painted green sunsets and people with green faces and red roses that were blue and yellow sand that was blue. He (or she)

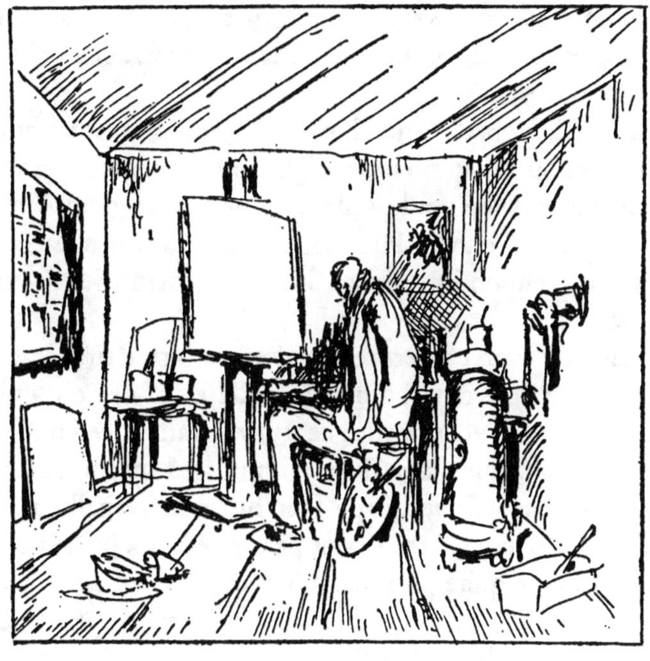

The modern painter is a free citizen—free to come and go at will—but he has nowhere to go.

pasted bits of horsehair on samples of homespun materials, on pieces of black cardboard and called it *The Soul of Democracy* or *The Triumph of Woman.* He pretended to despise pictures that meant anything at all as relics of a barbarous age when the soul of man had not been free. He presented us with the sort of scribbling that is done on the walls of a telephone booth by an impatient customer. He asked us either to accept his latest effusions as the spirit of the year 1938 or to stand revealed as artistic Tories and spiritual reactionaries. Just as he let all the factory sirens blow at one and the same moment to an accompaniment of hurdy-gurdies and then asked us to recognize the ensuing noise as a *Symphony of Labor.*

If he played his cards at all cleverly, he could always find a few critics willing to proclaim him as the latest prophet of the modern spirit and to poke fun at the rest of the world that was too utterly set in its old-fashioned ideas to appreciate these revelations of the new spirit of mankind.

Since the architect had turned his back upon the painter and now declared that pictures had no more right to be hung on the walls of a house than mirrors, he could only sell these strange looking concoctions to a few self-chosen initiates, and the most dangerous of all elements was thereupon introduced into the world of art—the element of snobbism.

I hope that you won't interpret this rather bitter tirade as an attempt to go back to the days before the collapse of our old universal culture at the end of the eighteenth century. I can indeed understand that a certain type of man is so deeply impressed by the unexpected sight of a sun-drenched landscape that his eyes actually receive a shock which makes him see the sky as pea-green or a brilliant scarlet. Such experiences are quite possible. They may never have happened to you but that does not mean that they cannot happen to others. All sorts of things can be said in all sorts of ways, by all sorts of men, provided they have the necessary technique to give a true expression of their innermost sensations. If you are a swimmer, you will know what I mean, for the perfect swimmer can keep himself above water in almost any sort of manner and way by moving only a few fingers or by wiggling his toes or sometimes by doing practically nothing at all. He does not have to follow the instructions of his teachers: fold your arms under your breast, draw in your knees. That part of his training has become a completely unconscious detail of his aquatic behavior, just as experienced painters or fiddlers can permit themselves all sorts of liberties and yet produce the desired effect. For like the swimmers, they have so completely mastered their technique that it has grown into an unconscious part of their very souls and bodies, or, as we sometimes express it, they "stand above their technique." The technique of course is there but it has now become their obedient servant while they have ceased to be its rather uncertain and somewhat balky slaves. I am now riding one of my pet hobbies—the hobby which you may remember from my book on the Arts—the supreme importance of a perfect craftsmanship.

The artist who is also the perfect craftsman can do anything he wants in any way that at the moment seems most desirable. But the artist who has not completely mastered his technique will fare as badly as the inexperienced swimmer. He will drown or withdraw from the catcalls of the audience.

Will the present situation, detrimental to both the artist and to the public at large, last forever? No, it won't; but it will last for a good many years to come. The importance of technical perfection is once more being duly stressed. But it will not be so easy to overcome our psychological handicaps. For we are living in an age of transition. We are right in the midst of the greatest spiritual, social and economic revolution the world has ever experienced. The old ideals are dead and the new ideals have not yet appeared upon the scene, which means that the old standards have been discarded and that no new standards have as yet been evolved which satisfy the sort of people we on this side of the ocean happen to be. In many countries of Europe a new set of ideals and therefore a new set of standards have been deliberately forced upon the populace, but that sort of method cannot be applied to us, for we still regard personal liberty (of both thought and action) as the greatest of our many privileges. We too need new ideals and new standards, but we will have to work them out for ourselves and in our own way or they won't be of the slightest use to us.

While this is happening, we can however prepare ourselves for that happy day by trying to understand why the artists of the past painted the way they did, in order that we may the better appreciate the painters of our own time when they try to solve the problems of the year 1938 in the vernacular of their own day.

NINETEENTH CENTURY

AMERICAN

George Inness (1825–1894):
Millpond, Art Institute of Chicago

James Abbott McNeill Whistler (1834–1903):
The Artist's Mother, Louvre, Paris
Falling Rocket: Nocturne in Black and Gold, Art Institute of Chicago
Portrait of Thomas Carlyle, Art Gallery, Glasgow

Winslow Homer (1836–1910):
The Gulf Stream, Metropolitan Museum of Art, New York

Thomas Eakins (1844–1916):
The Surgical Clinic of Professor Gross, Jefferson Medical College, Philadelphia
The Thinker, Metropolitan Museum of Art, New York

Mary Cassatt (1845–1926):
Young Mother, Luxembourg, Paris
Mother and Child, Metropolitan Museum of Art, New York

Albert Pinkham Ryder (1847–1917):
Toilers of the Sea, Phillips Academy, Andover

John Singer Sargent (1856–1925):
Portrait of the Misses Wyndham, Metropolitan Museum of Art, New York

DUTCH

Vincent van Gogh (1853–1890):
A Woman of Arles, Museum of Modern Art, New York

ENGLISH

Joseph Mallord William Turner (1775–1851):
Calais Pier, National Gallery, London
The Fighting Téméraire, National Gallery, London
Ulysses Deriding Polyphemus, National Gallery, London

John Constable (1776–1837):
The Hay Wain, National Gallery, London
Scene on the River Stour, Metropolitan Museum of Art, New York

Ford Madox Ford (1821–1893):
Work, Manchester Art Gallery
Dante Gabriel Rossetti (1828–1882):
Monna Vanna, Tate Gallery, London
Lady Lilith, Metropolitan Museum of Art, New York
Sir John Everett Millais (1829–1896):
Lorenzo and Isabella, Liverpool Gallery
Portia, Metropolitan Museum of Art, New York
Sir Edward Burne-Jones (1833–1898):
Cophetua and the Beggar, Tate Gallery, London

FRENCH

Jacques Louis David (1748–1825):
The Death of Socrates, Metropolitan Museum of Art, New York
The Coronation of Napoleon I, Louvre, Paris
Jean Auguste Dominique Ingres (1780–1867):
La Source, Louvre, Paris
Portrait of M. Bertin, Louvre, Paris
Jean Louis Théodore Géricault (1791–1824):
The Raft of the Medusa, Louvre, Paris
Jean Baptiste Corot (1796–1875):
Ville d'Avray, Metropolitan Museum of Art, New York
Dance of the Nymphs, Louvre, Paris
Morning, Louvre, Paris
Eugène Delacroix (1798–1863):
The Massacre of Scio, Louvre, Paris
Dante's Bark, Louvre, Paris
The Abduction of Rebecca, Metropolitan Museum of Art, New York
Honoré Daumier (1808–1879):
Republic, Louvre, Paris
Third-class Carriage, Metropolitan Museum of Art, New York
Gustave Courbet (1819–1877):
The Polish Exile, Metropolitan Museum of Art, New York
Pierre Puvis de Chavannes (1824–1898):
Legend of St. Geneviève, Panthéon, Paris

Camille Pissarro (1830–1903):
Bather in the Woods, Metropolitan Museum of Art, New York

Edouard Manet (1832–1883):
The Courtesan Olympia, Louvre, Paris
Déjeuner sur l'herbe, Metropolitan Museum of Art, New York

Edgar Degas (1834–1917):
The Rehearsal, Metropolitan Museum of Art, New York
Dancers Practicing at the Bar, Metropolitan Museum of Art, New York

Paul Cézanne (1839–1906):
The Blue Vase, Louvre, Paris
Card Players, Barnes Foundation, Merion, Pennsylvania
Landscape, Metropolitan Museum of Art, New York

Claude Monet (1840–1926):
Waterloo Bridge, Luxembourg, Paris
Haystacks in the Snow, Metropolitan Museum of Art, New York

Auguste Renoir (1841–1919):
Portrait of Mme. Charpentier and her children, Metropolitan Museum of Art, New York
The Ball at Montmartre, Luxembourg, Paris

Henri Rousseau (1844–1910):
The Jungle, Art Institute of Chicago

Paul Gauguin (1848–1903):
Spirt of the Dead Watching, Museum of Modern Art, New York
Self-portrait, Chester Dale Collection, New York

Georges Seurat (1859–1891):
La Grande Jatte, Art Institute of Chicago

Henri de Toulouse-Lautrec (1864–1901):
Le Cirque, Art Institute of Chicago

GERMAN

Hans von Marées (1837–1887):
Die Werbung, Neue Staatsgalerie, Munich

SWEDISH

Anders Zorn (1860–1920):
Self-portrait, Uffizi, Florence
Portrait of Mrs. Potter Palmer, Art Institute of Chicago

SWISS

Arnold Boecklin (1827–1901):

A Roman Landscape, Metropolitan Museum of Art, New York

AMERICAN

John Sloan (1871–):

Dust Storm, Metropolitan Museum of Art, New York

John Marin (1875–):

Wind on Land and Sea, An American Place, New York

Boardman Robinson (1876–):

Murals in Kaufman's Department Store, Pittsburgh

George Bellows (1882–1925):

Portrait of the artist's mother, Art Institute of Chicago

Edward Hopper (1882–):

Lighthouse Hill, Museum of Modern Art, New York

Rockwell Kent (1882–):

Deer Season, Art Institute of Chicago

Down to the Sea, Brooklyn Museum

Georgia O'Keefe (1887–):

Ranchos Church, Phillips Memorial Gallery, Washington, D. C.

Thomas Hart Benton (1889–):

Murals in the New School for Social Research, New York

Murals in the Whitney Museum of American Art, New York

Charles Burchfield (1893–):

Civic Improvement, Private collection, New York

Grant Wood (1892–):

American Gothic, Art Institute of Chicago

ENGLISH

Augustus John (1879–):

The Smiling Woman, Tate Gallery, London

FRENCH

Albert Besnard (1849–1934):

Woman Warming Herself, Luxembourg, Paris

Henri Matisse (1869–):
Girl in Yellow Dress, Ettie Cowe Collection, Baltimore
The Buffet, Luxembourg, Paris
Georges Rouault (1871–):
Circus Woman, Private collection, New York
André Derain (1880–):
Landscape, Museum of Modern Art, New York
Maurice Utrillo (1883–):
Montmartre Street, Chester Dale Collection, New York
André Lhote (1885–):
Les Dames d'Avignon, Art Institute of Chicago

GERMAN

Max Liebermann (1847–1935):
The Ropewalk, Metropolitan Museum of Art, New York
Lovis Corinth (1858–1925):
Self-portrait, Posen Museum
Paul Klee (1879–):
Romantic Park, E. M. Warburg Collection, New York
Franz Marc (1880–1916):
The Three Red Horses, Folkwang Museum, Essen
Oskar Kokoschka (1886–):
Portrait of Mme. la Duchesse de Rohan-Montesquieu, Folkwang Museum, Essen
Georg Grosz (1893–):
Cold Buffet, Art Institute of Chicago

ITALIAN

Amadeo Modigliani (1884–1920):
Nude, Chester Dale Collection, New York
Giorgio di Chirico (1888–):
The Great Metaphysician, Barnes Foundation, Merion, Pennsylvania

MEXICAN

José Clemente Orozco (1883–):
Prometheus, Pomona College, Claremont, California

Murals in library, Dartmouth College, Hanover, New Hampshire

Diego Rivera (1886–):

Murals in the Department of Education, Mexico City

Murals in the Stock Exchange, San Francisco

RUSSIAN

Vassily Kandinsky (1866–):

For and Against, S. R. Guggenheim Collection, New York

SPANISH

Ignacio Zuloaga (1870–):

Portrait of Daniel Zuloaga and his daughters, Luxembourg, Paris

Pablo Picasso (1881–):

Nude, Guillaume Collection, Paris

Mandolin Player, Art Institute of Chicago

Joan Miró (1893–):

Little Dog Barking at the Moon, New York University

www.ingramcontent.com/pod-product-compliance
Lightning Source LLC
LaVergne TN
LVHW050540100826
845148LV00002B/635